We Break Through

Dr. Kimberly Hayes

A GOSHEN PUBLISHERS BOOK   VIRGINIA

We Break Through
ISBN: 978-1-7378405-5-8

Copyright ©2022 Kimberly Hayes

Published in 2022 by:
GOSHEN PUBLISHERS LLC
P.O. Box 1562
Stephens City, Virginia, USA
www.GoshenPublishers.com

Our books may be purchased in bulk for promotional,
educational, or business use. For inquiries, please
contact the publisher via email:

Agents@GoshenPublishers.com.

First Edition 2022

Cover designed by Goshen Publishers LLC

Printed in the United States of America

All Scriptures are quoted from the King James Version
of the Bible unless otherwise noted.

TABLE OF CONTENTS

To everyone who has been broken,

do not die from the breaking.

Break through, instead!

THANK YOU

To my only sibling, my big brother, Redell Young, II, we have had some amazing reflective conversations throughout my entire life. You have always been there for me as my first best friend. I enjoy seeing you happy with Gina-Schmina and watching you be a father and grandfather—you are good at it. Just like every football game you have ever played, you still carry the ball well. Slow head nod!

To Pennie Summers and Wendi Smith, thank you for the regular conversations. When we get together, we check things off our goal lists, we check in to be sure we have a sounding board. I love our reflections. I have learned so much by watching both of you exhibit great strength in the toughest of times.

To Andrea McNealey and Yasmyn Southerland, you always reach out to me for advice, to vent, to laugh, and to have a healthy cry. You honor me by trusting me, and both of you have much wisdom to share. I love our reflections and what I see in you.

To ALL my cousins, no matter how near or far, no matter how long it has been in between our conversations, to my little cousins and big cousins, thank you for doing life with me. I am literally crying real tears as I think of each of you. As my cousins, you have been like siblings to my brother and me. You are like little versions of my aunts and uncles, little versions of our grandparents, as I see all their good traits and so much more wonderfully unique traits in you. To my bonus cousins, despite how or when in life you were added to my tribe, you are included in this appreciation as well.

To my Bestie, Stephanie Moore, in so many ways our friendship is a welcomed contradiction—a testimony for what is most important in life. Nothing stops you and I admire that. Just within these last few years, I have reached higher heights because of you—although, I still just want to sit in my office with the door closed! (Smile)

To Pastor Shawn Hines, Sr., I cannot even gather the words to express how much strength I have gained through our reflections and discussions. Whether we are on the phone or sitting near each other in the pulpit—you keep me cracking up. Everyone in ministry leadership should have a friend like you.

To all my goddaughters, I pray for wisdom, strength, fortitude, health, and wellness, and for you to know God and His great plans for your life.

Being in community with Goshen's GPubDelta for this second book was a bonus dose of awesome. Thank you, Dr. Shawn Richmond, for your obedience. Goshen Publishers is an amazing publishing company. Thank you to my editor, Sarah Lamb—I NEEDED you again and you NEVER drop the ball.

INTRODUCTION

We Break Through specifically deals with an individual's response to a break. This book will help promote healing and hope for long-term resilience against future breaks. We break though because it is a timely necessity. Through stories and discussion, We Break Through proposes that no matter where you are in your breaking experience, there is always a way to break through!

My vision for this book is for it to be an independent, yet collaborative read, before or after We Collide, my first book about relationships. We Collide discusses how to manage conflict resolution within relationships by defining offenses as collisions. It suggests that relationships can be born again to mirror God's redemptive plan for our individual lives within our relationships.

The purpose of this book is to dive deeper into what happens when we encounter dysfunction to the point of breaking. I want to explore some of the many ways an individual may break and how one break potentially creates multiple splitting paths. Although We

Collide addresses the individual, relationships, and community, it focused primarily on relationships. We Break Through will also address the individual, relationships, and community, but will focus more on the individual's path towards hope.

We were all whole at one time. Despite our various breaking experiences, we can be whole again. The breaks of life do not have to break us. There is hope for breaking through.

CHAPTER 1:
BREAKING BECAUSE OF COLLISION

ACCIDENTS!

A break is when something that was once whole is now divided into smaller parts because of too much pressure, deterioration, or by force.

As a child, we may have experienced disappointment after our favorite toy was broken or after finding a torn page in one of our favorite books. Perhaps it caused us to feel put off and frustrated that the thing we enjoyed so much may no longer serve its purpose to our satisfaction. In some instances, the broken thing may still be useful to an extent, but now requires some modifications and exceptions to be made for minimal enjoyment.

It would be like sitting down to play a game of Monopoly, but some of the money is missing. What do you do when you run out of money after only two trips around the board with four players? It is bad enough if the top hat, thimble, or iron tokens are not available for selection to represent your placement in the game. But now the money is low too? I mean, how can you really appreciate an intense game of chess if a queen is missing? The movements and the rules would still be the same, but a strategic play may not feel so powerful if a bottle cap was being used to represent the queen instead.

Disappointment is a natural response to any kind of break. Disappointment, in fact, is an appropriately healthy response to a break because it conveys that you are aware that something is no longer whole. It is an indication that you recognize the difference between being fully operational and dysfunctional. But when YOU are the thing that is no longer whole, and perhaps divided into smaller parts, you face a greater set of obstacles within the scope of your disappointment. You might be left wondering how you will manage your disappointment, let alone the potential disappointment others may experience when they either observe your brokenness or experience it firsthand by being in relationship with you.

I want to discuss the set of obstacles that we face when we are disappointed by having experienced some form of break. I want to identify the many ways in which our paths diverge when we are trying to recover. In doing so, we will have to investigate and discuss the cause of the break. Whether it was brought on by too much pressure, deterioration, or by force, it is the many splitting paths that stem from the original break which often contribute to the delay of our wholeness.

Whether we acknowledge it or not, when our wholeness is delayed, we are frustrated. These frustrations are compounded if the break or tear is never mended or resolved. Seeking closure is often underrated and misunderstood. While closure can certainly bring peace of mind, many times you may still be unsatisfied by how something ended. When you are looking for the reason why someone did something or are trying to figure out why you made a certain decision in your past, you may not get the responses you hoped for. But it is worth the effort to explore the twists and turns along your journey to reveal the strength, fortitude, wisdom, and new knowledge you gained as you worked hard to recover.

Whether the break was brought on by someone else's carelessness or that of your own, seeking a resolution is the healthiest action. Avoidance is a huge obstacle. In my previous book, *We Collide*, I discuss relational collisions and point out how brokenness can hinder personal growth and development. A collision is an offense that has escalated to unmanaged conflict, and from the examples presented in the book, we find that unmanaged or mismanaged conflict will push anyone to a breaking point. I am not trying to get you to never experience hurt at all, but let's not allow any hurt to push us so far that we feel as though we are broken beyond repair.

Let's begin with relational collisions as an obstacle. When an offense has escalated to unmanaged conflict, one of the biggest reasons why is because we do not want to do management in our relationships. Period.

In my other life as a senior systems engineer, I had a meeting with my immediate supervisor. She asked me if I had ever considered pursuing any line management opportunities within the company. Little did she know, for the past three years I had been asked that same question by other supervisors, co-workers, and close friends who work for the same company. They all said the same thing: you are good with people, you are a great motivator, you are detail-oriented, and you always have a positive attitude.

I am so grateful that this is what others see in me, both in the marketplace and in ministry. She continued to explain that with all her accolades, experience, institutional knowledge, and many requests to pursue higher management positions herself, she has never considered going beyond where she is because she does not want to do any more management than what she is doing right now. She does other things to leverage her expertise and fulfill her career goals like teaching on the collegiate level, writing technical papers, consulting, and has long since established herself as principal staff. So, when you consider her reluctance to do more management in this regard, it is easy to identify with her and say, "No", to more management. In fact, I absolutely agree with her perspective, which is why I have put off the pursuit of line management (until now, smile).

In relationships, however, you cannot dismiss the need for management, let alone the need for conflict management. Neither can you make management the sole responsibility of the other party. We must do management, and we must do it regularly. If we do not, we will be forced to do conflict management and if we treat that like we treat daily relationship management, then there will always be conflict and chaos leading to a collision. And for the people hiding in the back who have somehow managed to avoid the management of everything by sweeping it all under the rug, eventually, you will trip and you will bleed—or cause someone else to.

We need regular maintenance and that should be taken seriously. Otherwise, the negative stimulants that lead to relational collision including faulty communication, disappointments, and disaster will create such an emotional imbalance that a minor offense will be all that is needed to expose our brokenness and cause an unnecessary collision.

We may not be motivated because of the workload, but avoidance is tragic. Put the work in. Perform daily maintenance on yourself. Be an attentive manager of your current relationships. Step into management, collide less, and experience fewer breaks.

But what about other stressors that cause a different kind of break? What about a physical break in our bodies or an emotional break? With the amount of stress that we deal with daily, physical injuries can most certainly lead to an emotional break just as much as emotional burdens can lead to physical breaks. The mind and the body are connected. Mismanaging our emotional health can lead to a weakened immune system, leaving us susceptible to viruses and colds. When stressed, we are less likely to stay on top of our physical well-being, and depending on the urgency of our mental condition, it could lead to self-harm and fewer limitations in dangerous situations. Likewise, when experiencing a serious health condition, our ability to cope can be compromised due to stress and the extended use of certain medications.

Why do we break? We experience breaks in our lives for several reasons: too much pressure, deterioration, or by force. Oftentimes, breaks can occur when we are not prepared, when we fail to take good care of ourselves, or when we are injured by an outside force.

When we are not prepared, we break from trying to manage too many things on our own. The pressure that builds up from carrying far too much on our shoulders can not only weigh us down but also immobilize us and cause us to break from carrying so much weight. Where are the reinforcements? Have we rejected help? Have we convinced ourselves that nothing else and no one else is needed to complete the task?

Let's meet a young executive who experiences a break when trying to meet a deadline. He's a first-generation college graduate and has been waiting for the opportunity to move up in his company. He's a charmer with the clients, his personal life never interferes with his profession, he only vacations when the office is closed for the holidays, and he never ever takes a sick day. He is the first to arrive at the office and the last one to leave. Everything he touches is a sure win, but over the past few months he has developed some anxiety managing everything on his own.

As a child, he was thrust into independence extremely early when his father was laid off from a very good job as a line manager in the local factory, causing him to have to take on several lower-paying jobs. His mother no longer had the opportunity to be a stay-at-home mom. The young executive became the mother and father to his three younger siblings while their parents were out of the house for hours, making just enough money to keep them afloat. This young man became an executive long before he was professionally qualified, by getting everyone dressed and off to school every morning, assisting with homework, making all the meals, and keeping them satisfied with games, movie nights, and creative storytelling before bed. While peers were playing sports and thinking about who to ask to the next dance or party, he was doing all his homework during class time and getting home immediately after school to keep a regular routine for his brother and sisters, ending with bedtime at 8:30, just to have the last couple hours of the night to himself. He was adulting, long before he should have been.

He was often told that he was very strong, mature, and dependable. He felt like he had to keep on being strong, mature, and dependable because his parents and siblings needed him to be. There was very little room for failure, so he made sure failure never happened. He did not want to let his parents down and he did not want to see his siblings miss out on any of the attention and comforts they were used to when Mom was at home and Dad was getting his steady salary.

The young executive was getting the job done as a responsible older brother. This mindset followed him into every other area of his life. He went to a college near home so he could continue to be in his siblings' lives on a regular basis. Even though his parents were getting back on their feet financially by this time, he still felt he needed to be available. With the few friendships that he forged, he took on the same responsibilities—being the one who would always make things right, saving the day, doing what others would not do, and doing what he did not have to do.

The anxiety first began when he realized the newest managing partner was not all that impressed by his past achievements. It sort of seemed like he read his glowing file and then tossed it to the side. While there was nothing in the file that indicated the young executive had done anything wrong, there was also nothing in his file that indicated he had overcome any challenges in his career. The new partner was looking for growth, not just good reviews. Little did he know, the young executive had nothing but challenges his whole life.

Growing up before it was time to grow up, and with extra responsibilities, was difficult, but he knew what was needed—be like Mom and Dad when Mom and Dad could not be there. For his friends, it was to be the sounding board and the one who showed up to fix everything whenever they needed him to. That was selflessly unrewarding, but he was a pro at showing up. Now, as a young executive, he had to show up, please his clients, and prove himself to a new authority figure who was looking at so many others who were proving themselves too.

When we fail to take good care of ourselves, we neglect our foundation and the fundamental building blocks that allow us to function at our best, no matter what we are doing. When we arrive at a place where what we are doing is working, we must step back and take care of ourselves so we can continue to do more good things. Stepping back does not mean stopping or going in another direction. Stepping back simply means take inventory of where you are, celebrate your wins, do self-care, catch your breath, and fuel up for the next task. All machines need maintenance. All software needs updating. All instruments need fine tuning. We need regular maintenance too. The young executive learned how to do it all for others, but he never learned how to do what was necessary for himself. No one ever required this of him. Now, his body was about to force it to happen.

When the new partner joined the company, it threw the young executive off his game. Until then, he had mastered responding well to everyone else's demands. He thought he had proven himself and was aware of all the prerequisites for moving up. The new partner and his significant role in the young executive's daily tasks shook things up too much for him to continue business as usual. It made him uncomfortable. It made him feel like the little boy whose father lost his job, whose mother was no longer in the home, and whose younger siblings depended on him for everything. That little boy was overwhelmed with a heavy responsibility that came without warning. Now, with the first deadline approaching while reporting to the new manager, he was overwhelmed, anxious, and having to face feelings of not being ready or good enough—just like he felt as a young boy.

The young executive did amazingly well as a little boy with new responsibilities. In fact, he did well with responsibility his whole life, learning how to prioritize everyone around him, pleasing them, and performing for their benefit. But he did not do well making himself a priority. Neither was he even aware that his early adulting experience was traumatic, and he carried this unresolved trauma with him every day. Trying to out-perform the effects of the trauma is not the same as dealing with it.

When we are injured by an outside force, there is an unexpected interruption that not only stalls us but hurts us as well. There's no question that the early adult responsibility shaped the young executive in many positive ways. But when the pressure is too much to handle and there is very little room for error, little cracks begin to form in our foundation. These little cracks can go unnoticed for a long time, leading us to feel like all is well. But as soon as something happens that makes us feel the way we did when the initial cracks were created, we discover that the fissures have gained much ground and we are closer to a major break than we ever imagined. Sadly, in some cases, by the time we learn that an inevitable break is upon us, we may already be broken.

Perhaps right now, everyone who considers themselves to be tough as nails is saying, "I don't break. I never break." Keep reading, because we all experience breaks, and we each manage them differently. There are some very similar characteristics of those breaks that I intend to reveal in later chapters. A lot of us are tough, but there is plenty of room for us to learn how to recover better.

Besides, can we ever be too tough or too prepared to experience a break? A break can happen at any time, and it can happen to anyone. Even the most prepared person can and will be caught off guard. There is no way to know what will happen around the corner—and even if we had the foreknowledge, we still may not know how best to prepare or what the best response should be.

Being tough does not cancel or diminish a break. The toughest among us will find that their strength can and will be put to the test. In the case of the young executive, his anxiety continued to snowball until he had a full panic attack in the hallway just before a meeting. He was scheduled to meet with one of his favorite clients. But the new partner asked him to do something different when preparing the brief. He second guessed himself the whole time, but never reached out to anyone for assistance or reassurance.

On his way to the conference room, he felt his heart rate increase and his breathing become shallow. Before he knew it, the papers he carried fell to the floor as he dropped to his knees gasping for air. With tears in his eyes and very little strength to call for help, all he could do was wave his hands in the air hoping to get someone's attention. But there was no one to witness his emergency.

Thankfully, the new partner was coming out of his corner office just seconds later. Seeing the young executive in distress, the new partner picked up his pace and jumped into action. He squatted down to the young executive's level, draped one arm over his shoulder, and lifted him to his feet. The young executive could not walk, but the new partner was strong enough to steady his full weight as he moved him swiftly to his office. He laid the young man's body down on his sofa and called for his personal assistant to coordinate whatever urgent medical attention was needed. The new partner headed back out of the office, picked up the files from the floor and proceeded to conduct business as usual without the clients knowing what just happened on the other side of the conference door.

The young executive got the care that he needed, and once he understood how easily this could happen again, he continued to recover while adopting a few new habits. It turns out that he was simply afraid of failing and he was anticipating this failure the closer he got to his deadline. The presentation that was scheduled that day was the only thing that he could think about for weeks. Little did he know, the new partner was waiting for him to talk about the assignment and ask questions about the new direction he had asked him to take. He could see that the young executive had a promising future at the company and wanted to see how he could handle the pressure.

The new partner could see himself in the young executive and knew that he would be standing in his shoes before long. Instead of penalizing him for not communicating how the pressure was affecting him, he gave the young executive all the time he needed to recover, with pay and without worrying about his position. You see, when the new partner opened the folder that the young executive dropped while he was in distress, he saw that every report not only met his expectations but exceeded them exponentially. The clients were pleased with the new way their case was being handled and were more than happy to negotiate a bonus at the close of the deal.

The young executive may not have properly managed the trauma of his youth at the expense of his health. However, his collapse in the hallway that day was all the evidence he needed to learn how to ask for help, take better care of his body, and find someone to talk to who could help him manage his anxiety. The young executive not only got a positive review from the new managing partner, but he also got a much-needed breakthrough.

What happened to the young executive was an unfortunate incident, but it was not what one would consider to be a typical accident. Even with the added pressure put on him by the new managing partner, his collision was an internal one with himself. Technically, an accident is defined as an unfortunate incident that happens unexpectedly and unintentionally, typically resulting in damage or injury without a deliberate cause. We could probably say that for the young executive, it was an accident waiting to happen. Accidents happen! Something may be more responsible than someone. But when someone is involved, it can be situational and not even brought on by someone you know or are currently in relationship with.

The young executive could point to his parents for either asking too much of him at such a young age or for not seeing through his charade when he would say that everything was okay and he did not mind helping. His parents were far too caring not to be concerned about his well-being. They were so grateful for his willingness and maturity, especially since there was no other family to stand in the gap. In fact, once they learned what happened to him at the office and heard him finally talk about the stress from his adolescence, they were remorsefully apologetic. He was apologetic too, because he led them to believe everything was okay.

What if you never hear, "I'm sorry"? Your recovery is far too important not to manage when the guilty party is not sorry for the break they caused in your life. Your recovery is still necessary, even when there is no responsibility accepted by the guilty party or the consequences seem too lenient for the offense. What if there isn't a responsible party to blame and no "I'm sorry" to be given? You still must heal, and you must move forward beyond the break.

Let me share a story with you about a woman who was in a car accident. The roads were icy, and she was the passenger in a car that was sitting at a stop light. An approaching vehicle lost control over a patch of ice, forcing it into oncoming traffic. This pushed the sitting car into a light pole on the side of the road. Because of the road conditions, the driver of the sliding car was cautiously driving less than the speed limit before hitting the ice. However, the speed of the other cars trying to avoid the sliding one turned it into a projectile, making the sitting car its target. The woman was stuck in her seat and pinned to the pole until the fire department could free her from the cold icy trap, thirty minutes later.

Is the driver of the vehicle who lost control to blame any more than any other driver on the road under those conditions at that time? Was the driver of the oncoming car to blame? Was the passenger herself to blame for just being outside under those conditions? Everyone on the road took the same risk. It was an accident, and it could have happened to anyone.

The woman endured injuries that required several surgeries. The recovery interrupted her whole life. Recovery *became* her life. Her priorities no longer included nurturing and raising her family, good times with friends, growing as a professional, enjoying exercise, book club, travel, and running a travel blog online. The single priority was healing and recovery. Her single struggle was maintaining hope for a full recovery.

This recovery included receiving help through physical therapy, pain management, counseling for her emotional well-being, and financial assistance to recover lost wages due to inability to work. Each of these issues are included in her road to recovery because each issue represents a fracture as a result of the accident. Each issue is important because she is a survivor of that accident.

Had she died, there would be no need for physical therapy, pain management, consideration for her emotional well-being, or lost wages. Had she died, her loved ones would have to recover from her sudden death, and they may have to recover as she continues to heal from her injuries. In death, there is no more work to be done for the injured person. What does that tell you? It tells us that despite injury, as a living, breathing being, the work of recovery is for the living. Recovering is hard work.

By the simple fact that you did not die during or after your most painful break, there is a breakthrough that is available for you to experience. Recovery is not just about survival. The greatest recovery is being rehabilitated to a state of wholeness. The kind of wholeness that is worth fighting for, especially when breaking, is designed to convince you that wholeness is too far out of reach.

Hopefully, as you dive deeper into the following chapters, you will see yourself positioned to break through the collateral damage from the breaks of life.

There's a difference between breaking out and breaking through. It would be great to break out of some of the chaos in our lives. But for many of life's lessons, we should break through and not just out. Getting through things ensures that we fully experience a matter for maximum growth from lessons learned. Getting out, instead, may cause a lack of experience or growth that may require a redo sometime later.

Imagine a large family with several children under the age of ten, all stuck in the house on a snowy day. Now imagine the amount of pent-up energy if they are not allowed to go outside and play in the snow. If going outside is not an option, the alternative is lots of running around throughout the house. Parents, this is a scene that is all too familiar. No matter how many children you have, sometimes you must get them out of the house because the inside is not going to accommodate their needs. Depending on how many snow days there are, there will be only so many movies, snacks, and games keeping them occupied inside. At some point, there has to be a breakout.

The idea of making this change, while contained inside of a marginalized space, can be a difficult one without any foreseen end or victory. But to break through leaves you with the feeling that you went through it. You endured the challenge until the end. Not getting out of it too soon, and achieving the desired result which is to not only arrive at your next level of greatness but to arrive intact, is victorious to say the least.

We Break Through offers hope beyond the break. Just like the imagery captured on the cover of this book depicting many potential breaks immediately ahead of us on the road, we must not only focus on the beauty just up ahead, but also learn to accept that work, growth, and beauty continue to happen on our journey along the way. Only hope can keep you moving beyond the breaks to get to your breakthrough. Each chapter from the first to the last will help you adjust your perspective to see yourself beyond your breaking point and past the actual break to a new place of wholeness.

When a child breaks a toy and becomes disappointed in its loss of use, the main lesson learned is to take better care of your things. We need to take better care of ourselves, both before and after a break. The young executive learned to take better care of himself before he experienced another physical break. The woman in the car accident learned that while there was no one to blame, she and her family had to shift their focus to the recovery of her physical, emotional, and financial breaks.

The idea here is not to avoid the breaks of life, but not to allow life's breaks to break you. Hopefully, reading this book is either your first step in that direction or another one of many in that direction as you continue to break through and hope beyond every break.

Chapter 2:
Breaking Rejection

ACCEPTANCE!

Some breaks run deep when it comes to dealing with rejection. Whether it is a breakup, being turned down for an opportunity, or not being able to advance at a certain rate, rejection can be hard to experience.

Rejection is when something or someone is refused or dismissed. Despite the reason for the rejection, the rejected can experience negative feelings that could possibly last a lot longer than the memory of the actual rejection. Wow! How can this be? Rejection seems to have this masterful power to make you feel something that is not yours to feel and for an extended period. It is like carrying luggage that belongs to someone else for a trip that you are not taking. There must be some sort of smoke-and-mirror magic going on with rejection, and I hope to free us from its mysterious trance.

In this chapter, we will explore the hardships of rejection and how to decipher what is acceptable and unacceptable when dealing with the fallout of rejection. Before we can find hope after rejection and move beyond it, we must learn to deal with how it feels. Dealing with how rejection makes us feel requires that we are honest about what being turned down or turned away does to our confidence and ability to recover.

So, what does rejection feel like? Rejection can leave you feeling refused and dismissed. When rejected, you can feel as though you do not matter, like what you have to offer is not good enough, or as though you are not valued in any way. These are difficult feelings to manage because rejection gives the impression that we are being unfairly criticized and judged. It is in the feeling of judgment that we infer so many other things that may not be relevant to the rejector or their rejection of us.

Do you recall the sound of children arguing on the playground? Notice what happens once the argument turns into teasing and name calling. One of them is bound to say something crafty like, "I'm rubber and you're glue; whatever you say bounces off of me and sticks to you!" Well, that whole statement demonstrates the character of rejection.

While the rejector, let's call her Alice, initiates a breach in the relationship by pushing the other one away, the rejected person, let's call him Marcus, becomes the glue, not only absorbing the pain of the moment, but possibly, Alice's pain as well. You must be wondering, how in the world does that happen? If Alice releases herself from the relationship or denies the possibility of a new relationship, Marcus is left to deal with the shock of the moment. Marcus will wonder what has happened to Alice that made her decide to end it, while also dealing with his own feelings about being pushed away. I mean, after all, everyone was just playing nicely on the playground, and now this!

Alice is only one step ahead of Marcus, having either thought about her decision to end the relationship for some time or at least knowing what it is she will say about rejecting a new relationship with him just minutes before Marcus hears about it.

Whatever the time frame, Alice has the foreknowledge of what she will do or say. This foresight provides her some time to process her decision. But upon hearing about her decision, Marcus is perhaps so vulnerable in the moment that sometimes we become willing to take on all of the emotional charge at the time as our own; inquiring how Alice came to this decision, showing concern about her well-being, and all the while trying to process how he feels himself. This is the energy that makes any rejected person feel that the full weight of the matter was perhaps in their control, and therefore convinces them there was something they could have done differently to avoid feeling the way they do now. What a load to bear!

I find it interesting that in the moment of rejection, Marcus may automatically begin to wonder what it is that he must have done to warrant such a surprising break in the relationship. Yet, at the same time, seek to comfort Alice, who is currently rejecting him. An example of this would look like Marcus asking any of the following: "Alice, did something happen to you today to bring this on? Are you okay?", "Whatever you are going through, Alice, let me help you. You don't have to shut me out.", or "Alice, did I do something? Just tell me and we can work it out." Although Marcus is hurting from the possibility of being rejected, still, all he wants to do is help Alice. This is the part where Alice says, "It's not you, it's me!" Having said that, let me be very clear—if you are ever rejected in a relationship and you hear that phrase, ACCEPT IT.

Accept that the rejector felt it necessary to deny going any further so that whatever it is they must work out does not hinder you in the process. But do not accept the responsibility for their brokenness. Do not accept their pain, which led to why it had to happen the way it did or when it did. And for your own peace of mind, no matter how shocking it may be, do not accept their baggage as your own. When they say it is not you, it's them, believe them. Dry your tears and know that there is more for you down the road.

What if the rejection is not about a relationship at all? What if the rejection involves a job opportunity or gaining a potential client for your business? The circumstances are different, but the feelings can be very similar. The feelings of dismissal, being undervalued, or maybe not taken seriously, are still a lot to handle and could leave you feeling out of control and inaccurately judged.

Now, do not get me wrong—sometimes it is you. Sometimes it is us, and sometimes we should be pushed away so we can work on ourselves without hindering someone else in the process. Sometimes we do have to gain more experience for that opportunity or re-evaluate our pitch for potential clients. This chapter is not to shake a shameful finger at everyone who has to walk away, deny a relationship, or turn down an opportunity. A person who has rejected something or someone is not a bad person. Even though the way they said it or the actual situation itself can be carried out badly. This chapter is to help distinguish between what responsibility is ours and what is not, being on the other end of the rejection.

If you are not doing enough to sustain a healthy relationship, if you have not equipped yourself to be competitive in the marketplace, then do your research, find out what is required, open yourself up to new possibilities, do the work, and level up. Take that rejection as a lesson learned, add to your relational toolkit, add to your skillset, and go for it again. This is the time when the breaking experience should be accepted as a development challenge. See it as a very strategic path, albeit surprising, to get to the next level.

When there is a missed professional opportunity, instead of harboring disappointment, ask questions about what they were looking for, or what you could do to add to your skillset that would make you a more viable candidate next time. Even if you do not plan to seek a position with that company again, you will be much more informed when you seek employment elsewhere. This is how you overcome the emotion of the denial and deal with the issue itself. Not having enough experience is not a judgment of you as a person; it is a critical point about where you lack in skill based on their needs and your qualifications.

You might be saying, how is this not to be taken personally? Easy. You are not your skill. You are not your education. You are not just the experience you have gained or the lack of it. All these things are an extension of you as a person and what you have to offer, but they do not define your core being. If you had everything they were looking for, it would be a win for a new opportunity, but not necessarily a validation for who you are. If this was the case, then anytime you experienced a rejection, it would mean that you are worthless. The next time you experience a rejection, remind yourself that you are still valuable even if you are not ready for that opportunity. You are still valuable even if the relationship does not work out.

The act of rejection is so powerful that when you have been refused or denied, you ignore the actual object of the rejection and make it about you instead. In a breakup, your partner may be having trouble, but it is not your trouble. You are not necessarily being rejected. It could be the timing of the relationship or the realization that there are things that no longer positively align between the two of you. It is now up to the rejector to work out their trouble without you because it is not up to you to provide the solution or make the timing better. There is nothing left to do but take care of you.

In a missed opportunity, you may not have possessed a certain skill or certification, but it does not mean that you are not skilled otherwise. Whether this was an employment opportunity, a big break, a contract, a new deal, or audition, you are not necessarily being rejected. Even if it is the lack of talent, experience, or skill that is being sought after by those who are looking for someone to fill the spot, something did not fit. Now it is up to them to continue their search. But it is not up to you to force them to see something that they may have overlooked or is not there. Again, there is nothing left to do but take care of you and sharpen your skills.

Breaks in life stemming from rejection are disappointing, but they do not have to be defining. Do not allow rejection to define you. Let your response to the rejection be what defines you as a person. Let your continued commitment and effort to your craft speak volumes about your zeal and determination.

What if you had an opportunity for advancement, and it was shot down? In this scenario, it is still not you who is being rejected. It could be that your standards need tweaking. Perhaps they are measured by the wrong thing, are not necessarily focused in the right direction, or in alignment with their own. You are still worth the advancement, and if you get another opportunity to prove it, you should make sure you bring more to the table. There could be a measure of comparison involved, but it may not mean that you do not have "enough", you just do not have what they are looking for—YET!

Lest we are vain, we must accept that we are not everything to everybody—even in our best moments of peak performance. Whatever it is you are reaching for, keep on reaching and reaching. However, when you feel like you have reached a breaking point, instead of allowing rejection to break you, break the effects of rejection instead.

We can get beyond the breaks of rejection by accepting who we are before and after rejection to avoid either a mental or emotional breakdown. Apart from any dream job or the best relationship, know who you are, identify your qualities, and accept your flaws. I am not suggesting that you live your life expecting to be rejected at any moment. However, we must know that we are not in control of everything, and we cannot be what every other person needs. Sometimes, others have to work through their own needs as well as their own baggage in order to move forward. We cannot solve their problems for them. A rejection may hurt for us now, but it might be what they need to get better for themselves, without hurting you any further. Let them do their work!

This will help you deal with the realities of the break or rejection without allowing it to break you. Here is how:

Affirm who you are regularly. An affirmation is a positive statement confirming something to be true, or a positive statement that describes what it is you hope to become. By affirming yourself regularly, you activate your mind to think in that manner more often as you work to reach your goal.

Affirm who you are, separate and apart from the things you think define you (job, relationships, gifts, talents). Affirm your characteristics and traits.

There is still good in the break: freedom, self-reflection, and recovery. Good things can come from a break. For example, being released from an abusive situation. You do not have to endure that anymore—abuse is harmful and manipulative. It is not love (freedom). Having more time to see yourself without the shadow of someone else dimming your potential (self-reflection). Getting the much-needed space to heal and become whole (recovery). Sometimes a break can allow for personal growth and new opportunities that would have otherwise been overlooked.

It can be hard to accept that you must move on from a broken place that you did not create. An example of this would be a cheating or abusive partner, a job where the company went bankrupt, or there was a takeover, and most everyone is let go. This reminds me of a sad personal experience that I witnessed firsthand when a company that I worked for was taken over by a larger entity. Everyone knew about the acquisition but was promised that there would be no layoffs. After only three months into the merger, the new parent company realized they did not have a full understanding of the business that they acquired and determined that it was not going to be profitable to keep it as is.

One Friday morning, they called half the company into the large conference room. That half was given a severance package and let go immediately. The second half was given the opportunity to either leave immediately with severance or stay on for the next six months to rebrand the business and then leave with severance. There was no guarantee that anyone in the second group would be asked to stay after rebranding.

Thomas was in the first group. He was a big guy, a gentle giant and very nice to everyone he worked with. Unfortunately, he had been through a very bad merger like this about ten years before. He lost his family and home because he was not able to support them, and it sent him down a drunken spiral. Being laid off this time made him feel like a failure all over again, even though he had done nothing wrong. When he left the job that day with his severance in hand, he became so anxious and afraid that he committed suicide the following morning. Thomas did not create any of these circumstances, and he had been sober for over a decade. But he was broken nonetheless, and he could not see his way forward.

I hope you can see your way forward. If you cannot, let someone help you.

You are allowed to reject the negativity associated with rejection. You are allowed to eject from the pits of rejection. The pitfall of rejection is not your destination, and it should not destroy your life or your hope.

Chapter 3:
Breaking Things

ANGER!

Are you angry all the time? Do you have an angry resting face? Go take a look in the mirror to be sure. I will be here when you get back.

Did you see anger? What if you asked someone close to you if your resting face is often angry. Would they say yes? If the answer is yes to either question, then let's work on it. If not, let's work on it anyway because the introspection is worthwhile.

For all the strong and angry folks reading this, let me just remind you that reducing intensity just a little bit does not make you weak. Strength and anger are not synonymous. Anger typically causes a reaction when we attempt to gain control or try to shield our vulnerabilities. It is often the response when we feel we need to take extreme measures to protect ourselves or the ones we love. Despite the trigger or the reason for becoming angry, we can all learn to manage our anger better by changing anger's potential danger into determination or some other purposeful fuel.

I know some readers might be saying, "I'm not angry, I just have a bit of an edge". Being edgy is great, but being in a constant state of anger is not. What is the difference? Having an edge is equivalent to having an advantage over someone or being in a state of readiness in case something more is needed from you. Anger, however, is hostility or unfriendly opposition. Unlike edginess, anger is not just having an advantage or being prepared. It often causes an irrational response. Anger is a few steps beyond edgy, to where your response to most things is often unnecessarily overbearing or has a physiological outcome.

Anger or hostility is an extreme symptom of either loss, disappointment, powerlessness, fear, or any combination of these that has left us feeling out of control or vulnerable. Now, some others might be saying, "I'm not afraid of anything". But if we look at our constant need to defend or stand up for ourselves or others when there is no battle or offense, as if everything is a challenge daring us to prove ourselves, then it is because something or someone has convinced us that this should be our natural stance in life. The reluctance to learn how to stand differently could possibly be driven by the fear of what could happen if your footing is not this way all the time.

For this kind of person, having a gentler response is somehow inferior to the way we want to portray ourselves on a regular basis. Perhaps it is also because of a breaking or defining experience that we have convinced ourselves anger should be a representation of who we are and not just a reaction to a specific moment. This kind of disposition may feel natural, but it is not balanced. Chapter Four will talk more about disposition, but perhaps we can gain some equilibrium here too.

The compromising trait about anger is that it can lead you to a decision or action that you would not otherwise choose or perform. It can lead you to a lapse of judgment where you are justifying your anger: since he did that, now you must do this. Anger can be misleading, hence the saying, "cooler heads prevail". It is wiser deciding what to do next or how to act when there is a moment to breathe and regroup. Some of us need to take longer moments to cool off than others. Although anger can be invigorating and make you feel alive, it is only a temporary high that leaves you picking up the pieces when your response wreaks more havoc than the situation that caused you to become angry in the first place.

I want to share a personal, angry episode of my own that occurred about twelve years ago during a time when I shared an apartment with my brother. A situation happened and I allowed someone else's petty shenanigans to get the best of me. I knew they were being intentionally unreasonable, and I knew that I was allowing myself to fall beneath the aptitude of my character. Stay tuned, we will discuss aptitude and mental awareness more in Chapter Six. Although I kept it together while confronting the individual face-to-face and for the sake of my young son, who was in earshot, I did not do such a good job keeping it together after I was no longer being observed.

The agitator left and my son went outside to play. I walked to my room and the amount of anger was so overwhelming that I did not know what to do next. I could only make the decision to go to my room in an attempt not to involve my brother, who happened to be home. But the anger kept rising out of me like a forceful energy that could not be contained. I could not make any other decisions. I did not know what to do with my mind except run through all the nasty, foul responses that I chose not to say when I had the opportunity. These foul remarks flooded my mind, and I could not think clearly.

My body was also affected by this surge of anger. My hands flailed around, my arms swung back and forth. I paced for minutes around my bed and my eye sockets felt like fireballs. Each time I walked past my closet door I felt the need to strike it. Each time I walked the other way, I felt compelled to go back to the closet and face it. I did not know what to do with the physical urges overwhelming me.

Still walking back and forth around my bed, I felt the divisive energy daring me to release it, but I could not. I could not release these emotions, though I wanted to release them. I felt torn between wanting to unload the anger in a physical way and knowing that I should not. I felt torn between harboring an uncontrollable combustion and relieving myself with an explosive strike. I could not decide. So, I kept pacing around my bed in an L-shaped journey of confusion.

Make a left, walk towards the nightstand. Turn around, walk towards the bedroom door. Make a right, walk towards the window and the closet. Turn around, walk back towards the door. I wanted to pray, and I did. But prayer did not soothe me. I prayed in my head, but out of my mouth came cursing and unrecognized murmurings. My brother must have heard me talking out loud. I could hear him calling from his room, "Rev?" I did not answer.

This feverish spectacle continued until I could no longer keep myself from snapping and I found myself facing the closet as if it dared me to make contact with it. With burning tears rolling down my eyes, I released the tension. I released the anger, and I did not care what the aftermath would look like or feel like.

I could hear my brother walking towards my door, but he was not moving faster than my impulse. By the time he came in my room to see what the noise was all about, I had already taken my fighting stance and my fists were clenched. As he stepped through the door, I had just pulled my fist back from the first punch.

BOOM! I went in for the second punch. BOOM! With both punches, the closet door proved to be relentless. The only evidence of my punch was the loud rattling noise. It was not steady enough to absorb the whole impact. Just like a formidable opponent quick on their feet, the closet moved on its hinges, trying to avoid defeat. I felt mocked. So, I decided to go for the wall with the next punch. My brother caught me in full swing and trapped me with a bear hug so tight that I could not lift my arms anymore. All I could hear him say was, "Rev! Rev! Come on, Rev! Come on, don't do this. You're going to hurt yourself. Come on, it's not worth it. What's wrong? Calm down. I got you."

My brother hugged me close. Our bodies were caught in that embrace, and he had to move while I moved to keep me contained. I kept trying to connect my fist with the wall. Crazy yells came out of my chest like a beast who wanted to pounce but could not get out of their cage. My brother caged me, and I could not have imagined a better captor—someone who loved me and understood me more than anyone else in my life. I was certain that he knew this anger was not just about the current situation. He did not know what happened to incite my current rage, but he understood the kind of anger that had been developing inside us both since we were little children. This anger had a history. This anger was inherited. It did not originate with me, neither did it belong to me.

I will never forget this moment—the feeling of uncontrollable rage—no more than I will forget the feeling of my brother's love and understanding in his rigid embrace. This moment reminded me of a promise I made to myself a long time ago, after I had initially learned that anger and rage had rooted themselves down deep in my heart. I promised myself not to allow the anger to manipulate me like it had its original host and all the hosts after that. I promised not to unleash this anger on anyone else in the manner that I saw it unleashed as a child. I told myself that I would eventually be free from these unwanted emotions, but until then I would use the power they yielded for good and not evil.

I promised myself that instead of anger, I would have passion. I would be passionate about helping others reach their goals, to overcome their challenges, and find joy, and experience peace. This moment of anger showed me just how much power there was inside of me. Now, if I could only make good on my promise, I knew that whatever I set out to do would be fueled with passion and completed with purpose.

Is it okay to be angry? Yes, it certainly is. Even the Bible tells us to "be angry and sin not". Those five words assure us that there are times when we will feel annoyed and outraged by something or someone. Those words, coupled with the latter part of the same verse which says, "do not let the sun go down upon your wrath", caution us not to let our discord get the best of us to the point where our anger causes us to act out of character or become destructive in our relationships.

Now, here's the thing. When we do allow anger to take over, are we really acting out of character, or is that how we truly are? Aside from having a resting angry face, are we really angry all the time? Are we regularly frustrated that any little offense can take us to anger's darkest places? If this is how we really are, then anger has found a comfortable place of residence in our hearts. If this is the case, then something really is broken. We must decide to address it, otherwise we will be responsible for breaking so many other things, as well as other people, with the slightest spark.

What I find fascinating is that in some cases, we will never know or recognize how or when anger became our base reaction to everything, not just a warranted annoyance, offense, or threat. But having the courage to address our unbalanced anger despite its origin is worth it for our individual stability and that of our relationships as well.

So, how do we combat this need to be overbearing, to be advantageous far beyond edgy, or the need to respond to every annoyance beyond hostility? We must identify that we carry anger instead of expressing anger, and we must learn how to redirect the intensity in another direction worthy of great passion and focus. Admittedly, in the moment of anger, identifying the root and redirecting the emotion is hard to do, especially if we have already succumbed to a detrimental physiological reaction that we cannot undo—like punching the closet door and potentially hurting yourself, or worse, punching someone who is not deserving of your rage and hurting them for no reason. But if we seek balance when there is no offense, and remind ourselves that we cannot change the things of the past or other people, then perhaps that leaves room for us to handle any challenge with the level of response that is most suitable. This requires a measure of self-control.

When I reflect on the moments where I have felt a strong physical reaction to a situation, I realize that I have allowed anger to get me to a place where even if I do not physically react, the strong urgent feeling for destruction is still prevalent and it is not just below the surface. Evidence often shows that it has risen above manageable heights. You do not have to live with that turmoil inside of you, and the people who love you should not be forced to live with that turmoil either.

The promise that I made to myself during the bout of anger described earlier allowed me to shift my emotion and therefore shift the outcome. Even when my nature prefers to be overbearing, a shift is what is needed, not another seething gesture.

We can have this kind of self-control if we practice it. Anger management equips you with the right tools to either help you keep your cool as you learn how not to be so characteristically angry, or help you apply the appropriate energy to any given situation. There are methods that include counting, tapping, breathing techniques, recitations, affirmations, exercises, meditation, and journaling. These things give you the power to modify destructive behavior, knee-jerk reactions, and harmful impulses that will otherwise lead to further breaks.

Now, if you enjoy being this impulsive or you delight in the fact that people treat you as if you are a ticking time bomb, if you feel amused by this, then there is nothing I can say to convince you to dial it back a bit. But if you are done being manipulated by anger, if you are ready to have more control of your impulses, and mostly, if you are concerned by how your loved ones feel on edge as they navigate their relationship with you, then it is time to figure out just how to "be angry and sin not", or "be angry and destroy not" in a manner that works best for you.

Whether you were led to believe this is the way you should be all the time, or if hurt brought you to this place of uncontrolled emotion, a breakthrough is long overdue for you. Do not carry the baggage of anger with you one more step and do not pass it on. Passing it on will cause damage to either the ones closest to you or total strangers, neither no more deserving of the weight of anger than you were when it was put upon you. When anger is passed on to our loved ones, we are essentially training them that they can never or rarely be at ease when around us or engaging us. When passed on to total strangers, the offense can be like a thunderstorm coming upon them from nowhere. From that point on, for both the loved one and the stranger, there is no satisfaction or justice for what they endured when they encountered us in that moment. And guess what? The cycle continues.

While looping through this cycle of being angry, acting out in anger, and depositing anger into others, anger leaves you feeling as though there is no other choice. Please know that you absolutely have another choice—whether you choose it or not is up to you. You must develop the desire to rise above the destruction of anger and seek to exhaust all other alternatives.

The victory of breaking through anger is a victory for the past and the present. When you shift and choose to operate differently, when you release the need to be on guard in such a negative way on a regular basis, you overcome the moment anger attached itself to you, you overcome possessing characteristic anger, and you overcome responding angrily and inappropriately. This kind of victory has to mean more to you than anything else. It meets the need of the individual who is concerned about having balanced relationships and is aware of how their balanced behavior provides a positive charge to the communities they interact with and serve.

Now, how is it that community is a vital part of this conversation about anger? After all, in times like these where racism is prevalent and social injustices are afoot, couldn't the minority community and those who have been oppressed benefit from collective anger? Yes, certain issues disparaging minority communities should definitely be met with passionate participation, intense discussion, protest, and even aggressive efforts to change laws and bring attention to the ugliness of racism and oppression. But what it does not need is the unsteadiness of characteristic anger or the impulse of physiological anger, making it difficult to be seen and heard as equals, as opposed to being labeled as animals.

Let me be clear. Anger can definitely wake you up and cause you to become alert enough to respond to things that are broken. It is infuriating to be treated as less than human. Aside from racism, it is infuriating to be treated less than human in other abusive ways, as the list of society's ills is endless. Anger, sometimes, will make you decide that it is time to make an impact. Just do not let the fuel of anger fool you into creating a spectacle of the issue that needs more direct influential targeting and less dysfunctional destruction.

We will talk more about breaking through together in Chapter Nine. In the meantime, I want to challenge you to take the first step in overcoming your chronic anger by knowing and believing that there is a time for everything, including a time for every emotion; even anger. I would not want you to put this book down thinking that I want to do away with anger. Because righteous anger can and does have its place within reason, such as an injustice. Just know that we should do away with the crippling effects of anger's torment and manipulation.

The second step in this challenge is to know and believe that the benefit of breaking through is having enough hope to exceed the limited satisfaction of anger. Do not let anger turn you into something or someone held captive by an uncontrollable emotion. If you are struggling with anger, do not let it turn you into a monster. That is not your character, and it is not becoming of who God has created you to be.

Aside from our flaws, anger is a limiting manipulative fault that requires us to be accountable when it is out of control. There is a greater purpose for your life, and that purpose is in need of your passionate intensity. Lives will be changed when you redirect that energy. Those lives are counting on you and waiting for your change to come sooner rather than later.

Keep reading; there is more hope for breaking through.

CHAPTER 4:
BREAKING BAD

ATTITUDE!

Far too many times, we develop a bad attitude because of a break. This makes achieving our breakthroughs even more difficult. Not only do we have to contend with the break, but now we must also wrestle with our attitude towards the break and our attitude towards those who may be involved. Doing this while seeking our ultimate healing can be counterproductive. A bad attitude can disturb the growth process and distract us from our goals.

In this chapter, I describe the kind of attitude we should have when our focus is intact, provide help to eliminate our need to "break bad", and incite a desire for "breaking bad" in a more positive and productive way. First, let's peel back the layers of our attitude, and then let's learn what breaking bad should be.

Attitude is defined as a settled way of thinking or feeling about something or someone. Having an attitude about a matter means you have a determined perspective about it. Having a bad attitude, then, is possessing a negative perspective about a particular person or circumstance. Insert here the ideology of whether the glass is half empty or half full. Depending on your disposition, you may find yourself looking at the glass half empty if circumstances have left you wanting or in need, or you can look at the glass half full as an opportunity, despite your circumstances.

Moreover, attitude is not just how we think about something or how we feel about it. Our attitude is perpetuated and demonstrated through our actions for the world to view, experience, and judge.

Breaking bad is an expression of our attitude, especially when we are fed up and have reached a breaking point. The television series Breaking Bad portrays the life of a docile high school teacher who experienced a series of unfortunate events. These events ultimately incite a violent, immoral, and criminal response. He was pushed to the limit and became limitless in order to pursue the things he felt he needed and deserved.

Some of us have experienced these kinds of moments when we become so exhausted, overwhelmed, or frustrated by what we are going through that we become the opposite of our natural character. This is a very dangerous place to be in. The end result could mean losing our core values and thereby never reaching our greatest potential. Has something become so bad that we are willing to risk this kind of negative metamorphosis of who we are? Reaching a goal in an ill-mannered way is not the same as reaching the goal with your character intact.

Let me share with you a story about an eleven-year-old boy named Brady Houston who fell in love with a little girl whose family just moved into the newly built house across the street. Unaware that young love was budding in his heart, Brady watched the little girl as a team of similarly dressed men moved boxes and furniture from several trucks into the new home.

Brady could hear his mom in the background saying that they must be well off because the new family seemed to have the money to hire a company to do their moving for them. Brady's father chimed in with his agreement after having noticed the expensive vehicles parked on the street in front. But Brady didn't care about how much they might be worth or how nice their furniture and cars were.

All he was fixated on was the cute little girl in the pretty dress, with golden brown skin and a big smile.

This move took place late Friday afternoon. Brady was determined to meet her before the rest of the kids did on Monday morning at school. So, he asked his mom if they could do that neighborly thing where people showed up with cookies and gifts to welcome new neighbors. Consequently, it seemed as though Brady's suggestion was the solution to all of their inquiries, because Brady's mom wanted to meet the woman across the street carrying the fancy purse and Brady's dad wanted to meet the man who owned the nice cars. Now, you should know that Brady's family was somewhat wealthy themselves. But it was definitely strange to them to see another wealthy African-American family in such close proximity in this neighborhood.

Within the hour, Brady's mom had put together a basket of freshly baked chocolate chip cookies, a pitcher of freshly squeezed lemonade, and a neatly typed list of emergency numbers, amenities, entertainment, and recreation places that she thought the family might find useful as they familiarized themselves with their new neighborhood. Just before Brady and his parents left the house for their adventure, Brady's dad was sure to slip his business card into his pocket to present it at the right time. Brady's older brother, Ben, had no interest in what was going on across the street. Although, he did look once or twice to see if this little girl that Brady was smitten with happened to have an older sister. Since there was no older sister, Ben didn't think it was worth his time to be part of the welcome committee.

The curious Houstons set across the street hoping to make a good impression, but also hoping to forge a new friendship. The cookies and lemonade were a big hit, and everyone got along with each other extremely well. The families had a lot in common and even though the new family had more work to do to settle in, they could not help but jump at Brady's mother's invitation to come over later for a home-cooked meal. They were tired, but they were also very hungry.

While Brady's mother cooked and his dad stocked the bar and mini fridge with beverages in his basement man-cave, Brady went directly to Ben's room to tell him all about the little girl he met. Her name was Sara Jane Robinson. He was annoyingly infatuated, to say the least, but Ben was sure to give his little brother all the attention he needed, seeing he was already making plans to make her his girlfriend. When Brady finished telling everything, Ben's only advice was to be himself. He said it more than once for emphasis, and reminded his little brother that he had a great personality and anyone would be happy to be his friend. Perhaps Ben should have said, "be yourself" a third time. Brady had friends, but he wanted a girlfriend.

The dinner and the weekend flew by with the Houstons and the Robinsons getting to know each other. Brady and Sara Jane made a promise to find each other on Monday as soon as homeroom was over. In Brady's mind, Sara Jane was already his girl. He just had to let Sara Jane know how he felt. He had so much fun getting to know her over the weekend. Not only was she pretty, but she was very nice, smart, and athletic.

Unfortunately, Brady's love story played out just like it always does in the movies—things did not go according to plan. He and Sara Jane had a wonderful time when it was just them. But as soon as she got to school, everyone wanted to know who the pretty new girl was. Whenever Brady would get her attention, someone else would walk right up to her and shoot their shot. Can you believe it? Other boys asked her to the dance, to go get ice cream, or to hang out with them the following weekend. They asked her these questions right in front of him. How did they know that she wasn't actually with him already? Sara Jane could be his girl, but they disregarded his presence altogether.

By the end of the week, some of the guys cornered Brady in the gym's locker room and started asking him about her directly. Turns out, they did notice that he had been walking with her between classes and that they always got on and off the bus together. One of the boys asked, "Do you like her?" But Brady was caught off guard and felt embarrassed by his true feelings.

His response was, "Nah, she's not my type." This could not be any further from the truth. Not only was Sara Jane his type, but in the back of his mind he had already been referring to her as "his girl". He did not know why he did not speak up. He had always been confident, although not as rowdy as these other boys who lived in the lower-income neighborhoods nearby. He could have easily said, "Yes", or "No", or anything besides, "She's not my type".

Brady was disappointed in himself. Rowdy or not, he still felt he had the advantage since she lived right across the street. Brady's remorseful contemplation was interrupted by the guys jabbing each other declaring that they would be the next one to talk to her. Brady knew then, that he had to talk to her soon.

However, it took almost no time for Sara Jane to hear what Brady had said in the locker room, and of course it caused her to think twice about how much time they spent together over the weekend and how she was beginning to feel about him. She thought he was handsome and very kind. He was not like the other boys in the school who were somewhat aggressive, loud and rude. For the remainder of the day, she did not wait for him between classes because she felt hurt and confused by what she'd heard. Whenever he did catch up with her, she ignored him. When it was time to go home, Brady thought he would get a chance to find out what was wrong with her on the bus ride, but Sara Jane would not even sit next to him in their usual spot. As she walked past him to sit next to someone else, she looked at Brady in disappointment and said, "I guess since I'm not your type, I should find someone else to sit with."

Brady's attitude towards Sara Jane changed in an instant. He still liked her and thought she was the prettiest girl he had ever seen. But he could not stomach the fact that what he had said earlier, out of embarrassment, had gotten back to her and that it was affecting her this way.

When he looked back to see who she was sitting next to and saw that it was one of the guys who was in the locker room, something in Brady snapped. He knew he had so many opportunities to tell her how he felt over the weekend and during the school week, but he was afraid. He could have asked her to be his girlfriend. He could have told her that she was pretty. Instead, the boy she sat next to turned to her and said, "You're Sara Jane, right? I've been noticing you all week and I have been wanting to get to know you. Do you have a boyfriend?"

Wait! What? Just hearing someone else say the things he wanted to say infuriated Brady. He turned around and said as loud as he could, "NO, she probably doesn't have a boyfriend, she's too ugly to have one. I don't know why everyone keeps falling all over her anyway. She's shaped funny and she's stupid." He finished his rant by teasing her in a sing-song way, "Sara Jane is just plain Jane!" A few other kids on the bus did not miss the chance to repeat the teasing song, "Sara Jane is just plain Jane!" Then, of course, people started to laugh. Sara Jane did not laugh, she put her head down and the boy sitting next to her, who was confused by Brady's outburst, took the opportunity to whisper something in Sara Jane's ear that made her smile.

Brady could not believe she was smiling at the other boy. He could not believe the other boy was now her "knight in shining armor". He could not believe he created that moment for someone else to benefit from. Now Brady was no longer the nice guy. He was misunderstood and suddenly became the mean guy. Although Brady treated Sara Jane like a total stranger for the next few years, he never stopped staring at her every day from his living room window, wishing things were different.

Maybe you can relate to the way Brady's reservations turned into regret. When he could not pull off something that seemed so easy to every other boy who was smitten by Sara Jane's kindness and beauty, his attitude turned sour towards her. Within a matter of days, Brady presented a multiplicity of personalities that no one saw coming.

I would not necessarily describe Brady's experience as the kind of break that would scar him for a lifetime, but it would be memorable—it should be memorable. We will not get everything we want when we want it. Sometimes, what we think should be ours is not even for us, and when something is truly ours, we may go about obtaining it the wrong way. Separate and apart from any break is how we respond to the break and how we respond to those involved. We do not have to allow the break to diminish who we are or deter us from our goals.

There are a few things that Brady could have done differently. He could have been forthcoming with Sara Jane at any time during her first weekend in the neighborhood. Then, after her first day of school, he could have told her how he felt, seeing that every other guy was not hesitating to do so. He could have been more intentional in his response when he was asked if he liked her. He could have said anything besides "she's not my type".

When he realized she had heard what he said and was put off by it, he could have waited to talk to her after they got home. Brady had so many options, but he allowed the possibility of not having the relationship with Sara Jane that he had imagined get the best of him and it was demonstrated in his attitude. Brady's attitude was negatively expressed in an uncalled for breaking bad moment that lasted for a few years. Had he kept his focus on the prize, he would not have allowed a minor setback to change his attitude and undermine his authentic self.

Remember when I said earlier that a bad attitude can disturb the growth process? Well, Brady encountered a growth opportunity and his negative attitude caused him to miss a critical moment to grow beyond and despite his frustrations. That moment where he realized what he said in the locker room to keep his true feelings to himself was the exact thing that shifted the way Sara Jane felt about him, when she heard about it. Instead of taking responsibility for his own words, not only did he continue to pretend that there was no attraction there, but he carried a pretense of dislike for quite some time afterwards.

Brady's scenario may seem adolescent to you. But what about when it is us and the circumstances are a little more serious? What about when we act out in a way that is hurtful to ourselves and others? Because of his attitude, not only did it appear as though the thing that Brady wanted was no longer in reach, but the way he demonstrated his frustration revealed a character trait that was not typical of his true self. Rather, his impulsive breaking bad moment on the school bus seemed to define him more than his well-known all-around good guy persona. As adults, we already know that one hundred wonderful things can be easily forgotten by a single bad one.

As a leadership developer and mentor, I often encounter people in entry-level positions who want to elevate and expand their roles and authority. They are sometimes so anxious to get to the next level that they are willing to bypass their own personal growth. They are ready to learn content. They are ready to study methods and principles. They are ready to do all the work that they can be seen doing. But they are slow to work on their emotional balance and character development—you know, the things people do not typically see. People tend to want viewership, not necessarily leadership. Little do we know, it is the holistic preparation of a leader that readies us to operate in the higher levels of authority and leadership.

At times, it may be hard to overcome the need for an attitude adjustment, especially when we are not ready to be accountable for our actions. The danger in avoiding the work on our attitude is the longer it takes, the more we feel justified in our rash behavior. There is nothing wrong with being fierce and intense, but there is no excuse for our own faultiness, laziness, or acting haphazardly. For the professional who desires to move up in their career, this would be a practical lesson to learn. They may want to be seen, but they will never be respected unless they do what is necessary as well as suitable to achieve their goals. As for Brady, I would offer a quick review of Psalm 139:14, which reads, "...I am fearfully and wonderfully made, marvelous are thy works; and that my soul knoweth right well." Knowing how we were made, in our core, should remind us that we are built with resilience and strength. Be confident and strong as you breakthrough. Even though years went by operating with an attitude that was clearly not who Brady was, it would certainly take strength and courage for him to make amends for a cruel outburst that changed the course of his friendship with Sara Jane.

Making the adjustments to our attitudes will not yield immediate results, but the shift that occurs from the continued work is worth it for our own personal growth and for the benefit of those who are in relationship with us.

CHAPTER 5:
BREAKING TIME

AGING!

Can you believe that some breaks will have you questioning your age and existence? You may even have second thoughts about the very things you were once so sure about and what you know to be true. Growing older can be tricky. Even when you are at your healthiest, aging can offer some frustrating blows to your self-esteem. The audacity of a break when it tries to destroy your sense and sensibility!

Let me introduce you to Rose. Her story of overcoming the aging process may bring you hope, no matter how old you are.

Rose Dreyfus is beautiful, confident, elegant, intelligent, and had been married to her husband for fifty years. Now, at the age of seventy-two, she's been a widow for nearly two months. Not being married is still strange to her because marriage is all she's known since she was seventeen. Becoming a widow for the second time does not make the experience any easier. You see, Allen Dreyfus was Rose's second husband. In fact, Allen and

Rose were each other's second marriage. Years ago, before they were married to each other, they were both married to two people who were shot and killed in the same 7-Eleven store robbery in Prince George's County, Maryland. Nothing could have prepared either of them for what happened during a quick stop for coffee.

A robber entered the convenience store early on a Saturday morning, with the sole intention of stealing anything he could fill his book bag with. Still hungover and high from the night before, he was rather clumsy and brought great attention to himself when he knocked over a whole display of potato chips. Not only was he now very noticeable to the cashiers, but also to most other shoppers in the store.

In his effort to grab more snacks and candy before leaving in a rush, the robber bumped into Rose's husband unintentionally and was spooked enough to draw a weapon. Everyone nearby was immediately stunned and began to duck down after one of the cashiers yelled, "He's got a gun!" But immediately afterwards, Rose's husband yelled, "Keep cool. Everything's going to be alright. Right, Josh?"

Rose's husband recognized the thief after they bumped into each other. They worked the night shift together at a warehouse the year before. But Josh was startled to hear someone call his name. The hand holding the gun began to shake and Josh tried to walk backwards towards the door while studying Rose's husband's face for familiarity. At the same time, Allen's wife was just realizing what was going on as she walked towards the counter removing her headphones and seeing everyone standing still. She stopped right behind Rose's husband.

Just as Josh was about to open the door with his other hand, someone coming into the store opened the door before Josh could grip the handle. Josh lost his balance, stumbled backwards, and the gun went off, hitting Rose's husband in the heart, Allen's wife in the lower left lung, and another shopper in the arm. One bullet, three victims, two immediate deaths.

The shopper who was struck in the arm was Reverend Thomas Miles, a young pastor of a new local church, Walking by Faith Christian Fellowship. Pastor Miles offered to perform the funerals of both victims, free of charge. Allen and Rose grieved separately. They buried their young spouses separately. But it was not until they both received an invitation to attend grief counseling from the same pastor who shared in their tragedy, that they met for the first time.

Allen and Rose stood out from the rest of the group during their grief counseling sessions because they were both so young to be grieving the loss of a spouse. They were both silent for weeks, not able to understand how they could end up where they were so soon in life. But knowing that Pastor Miles was there during their spouses' last moments made them feel connected to him and his church.

Eventually, they began to talk and share fond memories of their young love. It was amazing how similar their stories were beyond the tragic day at the convenience store. Stories of falling in love, defending their love, and marrying young. It was not surprising that in a year they had fallen in love with each other. Despite their grief and pain, they had found something special, and it was clear to everyone in the church that God and love had smiled on them again.

Of course, Allen and Rose's families were hesitant, thinking that it was just their grief making them feel this way. They thought the two were too young to have been married the first time around. But just like before, there was a genuine connection. A mutual respect. A bond that seemed a lot more mature than their years. There was an understanding that everyone could see. They saw love. Again!

Rose never wanted for anything for fifty years, and Allen never needed anything else but Rose. They had a great partnership. The only other sadness they endured besides burying their first spouses, was that they never had children of their own. But they were the best aunt, uncle, and godparents anyone could ever ask for. Rose was sure about love, relationships, respect, and trust. What she knew to be true was her faith, her church, pastor, family, and friends. Her life had not been perfect, but she was perfectly happy with her life.

Now, after almost two months without Allen and despite the love of family and friends, Rose felt loneliness for the first time, and it was heavy. She had always been with someone, near someone, or serving someone.

Just before Allen and Rose got married, they decided to join Walking by Faith Christian Fellowship, the place where they had received grief counseling. Not only had they fallen in love with each other there, experienced their healing there, but they were drawn to the new young pastor who was just a few years older than they were. It gave them peace, knowing that Pastor Miles was there to pray over their spouses as they took their last breaths. He was also there for the new couple throughout their whole marriage. Over time, both Allen and Rose served in many capacities, including the choir, the usher board, and the finance team.

After Allen died, Rose took a short break from her long-term responsibilities at the church. But when she got back into the swing of things, she felt different. Rose felt off-balanced and was wondering if she would ever feel normal again. She brushed the feelings off and tried to remember what she had learned in grief counseling so many years ago. She prayed more and practiced self-care.

When Rose assumed her role as a lead trustee, it was just in time to meet a visitor who was a transplant from New York, named Sharon Ross. Sharon had started a new job and recently moved in with friends who lived near the church, until she could find a place of her own.

At first, everyone thought Sharon was a family member of Samuel Keys, another senior member of the church whose young adult nieces and nephews always came to visit. Mister Sam was seen talking to Sharon on a few occasions, but he was just meeting her for the first time, like everyone else. However, when Rose returned from her break, she and Sharon connected, easily. They talked about the church a lot, but also their personal lives. Rose learned that Sharon had been in the military and had recently suffered the loss of her husband about a year ago. Sharon was soon coming to Rose's house for tea in the afternoons and home-cooked dinners in the evening. Sharon attended church services more often—always showing up at the same time as Rose and sitting next to her on many occasions.

Rose thought that Sharon asked a lot of questions about her deceased husband, Allen, but Rose assumed it was because she could relate to having a deceased spouse. Despite their age difference, Rose felt they had a lot in common. Soon, Sharon started bringing lunch to her regular daytime visits with Rose, insisting that she somehow repay Rose for her kindness. Little did anyone know that the lunches Sharon brought to their tea parties were nothing like the sandwiches and dinners Rose had been providing. The food Sharon started feeding Rose contained a cocktail of sedatives, depressants, and poison that not only made Rose sleepy but started making her sick.

All this time, Rose felt she had found someone who not only understood what she had been going through, but someone she thought she could mentor and provide some guidance for, like the daughter she never had. In addition to working through her lingering grief, Rose had started to feel isolated when she took the break from attending church and her ministry responsibilities. So, when she came back to church and met Sharon, she felt like she had purpose again.

After a few of these lunches, Rose found herself waking up having lost track of time and wondering what had happened to make her feel so sleepy. Whenever she would follow-up with Sharon sometime later, Sharon would tell her that they had lunch, did girl talk as usual, and that all was well when she left. Eventually, Rose noticed money missing from her accounts and purchases on her credit cards that she could not explain. When she told Sharon about it, she was just as shocked and concerned as

Rose was—just like a good friend would be. But noticeably, after sharing this revelation with her, Rose started hearing less and less from Sharon and found it strange that her new daughter-like friend was hard to reach.

Rose decided to make an appointment with Pastor Miles not only to talk about her financial mystery, but to get some counsel about how she had been feeling emotionally since the death of her husband, and of course, her on-again off-again sickness.

On the day of her appointment at the church, Pastor Miles received a call from one of his pastoral colleagues. For the duration of the phone call, Pastor Miles' demeanor slowly changed from an initial satisfaction at hearing a friend's voice, to curious, to surprised, and finally to sadness and disappointment.

Pastor Miles' friend shared with him an incident where one of the seniors at his church befriended a new visitor who eventually drugged the senior and stole money from them. That was why he was calling his friends. He wanted to share the incident so they could be aware. While Pastor Miles waited for his friend to send over a copy of the police report and pictures of the perpetrators, he went out to greet Rose and bring her back to his office for their meeting.

Shortly after Rose began updating Pastor Miles about what she was experiencing, he was shocked that she was describing the same scenario his friend just shared with him. Just when Rose asked if he had seen Sharon lately, Pastor Miles got a text with Sharon's picture, along with a few other people that he did not recognize.

Sharon was not who they thought she was. In fact, that was not even her name. This woman was a criminal whose sole purpose was to get as much money as possible from unsuspecting people. She warmed up to the ones who were the easiest targets, like older people at churches and faith-based organizations. People who find it enjoyable sharing their life stories and history. Meanwhile, everything she shares about herself is a lie. She said she was in the military because she had learned that Sam was a veteran, and he was one of her targets. She said she was a widow because she had learned that Rose was a widow. There was nothing real about her. Her plan was that by the time anyone realized she helped herself to the bank accounts and credit cards of these senior victims, she was long gone to the next church.

It was in this moment that both Pastor Miles and Rose thought they needed to contact Mister Sam to see if he had become a victim too. Unfortunately, it would be sometime before they found out that Sam was a victim. Hours before they called, one of his nieces found him unresponsive in his kitchen and he had been admitted to the hospital.

This revelation left Rose feeling just as low as her current grief. She felt like there were certain cues she should have recognized. She felt angry, responsible, and useless. Not only was her grief distracting, but her aches, pains, and random moments of doubt had undermined her ability to comprehend the scheme Sharon had devised. Upon hearing all that this woman had done, knowing that she could have eventually become as sick as Mister Sam, Rose could not contain her tears. Pastor Miles prayed with her and promised to get her the help she needed to recoup her losses, but none of that made her feel any better about being a victim.

No one heard from Rose for weeks. Pastor Miles and several others tried to reach her, but she shut down and refused to be seen or communicate with anyone besides a quick text here or there to say that she's okay.

But she was not ok. Rose felt like giving up altogether. She was so low in spirit, she began to ask God why did He not take her when He took Allen. In this very moment, all she wanted was to close her eyes and wake up with Allen.

One day, she closed her eyes, and when she opened them again it was hours later and Pastor Miles was sitting next to her on the sofa, holding her hand and whispering another prayer. Rose is immediately confused as to how he was able to get in. Her pastor tells her that Allen gave him a key to their house last year when he first realized he was terminally ill. When Pastor Miles told her that Allen wanted someone that they both trusted to keep an eye on her, she looked up to the ceiling and began to laugh. This was not the answer she wanted when she prayed and closed her eyes, but she was almost willing to accept that it was the answer she needed for now.

Pastor Miles tried to convince Rose that she needed to go to the hospital to be checked out, but Rose would not consent. He begged her to let him contact one of the ladies from the church to come sit with her, but she contested that too. When Pastor Miles did not feel comfortable leaving her alone, he argued that either she had to go with him to church for his evening meeting or let him drop her off with a friend. Rose agreed to go with him to the church, but she did not feel good about having to be watched like a baby.

After entering the church, Rose sat in the back of the large sanctuary and watched as Pastor Miles approached a group sitting in the first few rows. The scene looked very familiar. He was about to begin a new grief counseling session and Rose could not shake the overwhelming feeling that this session could not carry on without her. She argued with God and told Him she did not need grief counseling again, but her spirit kept hearing that she needed it now more than ever. Rose heard a still small voice telling her to go talk to the class. She even felt a soft nudge on her shoulder, which caused her to turn all the way around to see who was nearby. She saw no one, but she felt God.

How could she talk to this class? She needed hope to recover herself. She needed time to recover. It was just a few hours ago that she felt like she wanted to die. It did not make sense to Rose that as soon as Allen died, she not only felt alone, but she felt her senses were deceiving her in ways that she had not realized before Allen's sickness and death. Neither did it make sense to Rose that her sensibilities or her ability to operate with a level head were no longer dependable.

She knew that God had given her and Allen to one another for the remainder of each other's lives. But now that he was gone, she felt that there was no more living to do. That is, until Sharon had made her feel as though she had something to offer. Rose wanted to die from the embarrassment of being taken advantage of. Instead of feeling wise in her seventies, she felt naïve in her old age. But there was no time to die, only time to heal and help others.

Rose prayed a quick, silent prayer from the back of the sanctuary. Then she looked up at the ceiling and told God, "I hear You, loud and clear, and I thank You for another chance to serve You." With that, Rose got up from her seat, walked all the way down the aisle, and joined Pastor Miles in front of the class.

The first thing Rose said was, "Years ago, I sat where you are seated. Here is where I recovered from the death of my first husband. Here is where I met my second husband, Allen. And now, here I stand as a widow once again." Rose shared her experience as a grieving widow, as a senior who now had to learn how to do life differently, and also as a recent victim of a crime.

This is Rose's story, but it is not a story of grief. It is a story of vulnerability. She knew grief, and she allowed herself to be open enough to connect with others in their grief and walk with them through their various and unique experiences. Rose resigned from all her other ministry duties, received formal training as a grief counselor and assisted the grief counseling ministry in any way that she could. Rose learned that there is still usefulness as you age. There is still a wealth of wisdom to utilize and grow from. It was not over for Rose. It was not her time to expire. Instead, it was her time to expand and explore.

CHAPTER 6:
BREAKING KNOWLEDGE

AWARENESS!

I often pray, "Lord, please keep my mind", when I am dealing with a break or when I am overwhelmed with life in general. What is your prayer when you are overwhelmed? Write it here before we continue, and we will come back to it later.

_____

_____

_____

_____

_____

_____

_____

_____

_____

_____

_____

In an effort to practice giving my all to God, no matter what I am going through, I strive to hand over the faculties of my mind to Him as the first fruit of my transition towards balance, healing, and wholeness. I believe we need God's hand in everything concerning us. As believers, when we yield our minds to Him, we are sure to do better at navigating the negative thoughts that keep us stuck during and after a break.

So, what does it mean to yield your mind to God? This chapter will hopefully help you do just that. When I say that we should be "yielding your mind to God", I am describing an intentional practice of letting God into our current state of mind and allowing Him to not only insert His perspective of the matter, but to interrupt our thoughts with His instruction and guidance. To yield in this manner is to have a steady awareness of God's readiness to lead and provide.

Right now, every professing disciple of Jesus Christ should be asking, "But shouldn't we already have Him on our minds to this degree already?" Yes, we should. But we often do not because of life's many distractions. Even when we do, we tend to lose sight of this awareness when difficulties are surmounting. It takes great effort to keep our minds only on Him.

Working at having a steady awareness of God through our most difficult times, especially when reaching a breaking point, means to seek him for decision making, gaining knowledge, gathering resources, increased understanding, and achieving peace. This is the work of a renewed mind. Breaking through difficult times calls for a **renewing** of the mind, as described in scripture—not just a one-time renewal, but a daily ongoing effort.

The Bible teaches that we should not do things as the world does, which includes the way we think about matters or how we process them. In fact, in Romans 12:2, we learn that we can avoid conforming to the ways of the world by having a renewed mind for the purpose of proving that God's will is good, acceptable, and perfect. It is beneficial to note that this verse falls under the heading for dedicated service unto God. How about that? This is a huge part of our work unto God—our demonstration of faith, worship, and acts of honor include how we render our thoughts and yield our minds to The One who can mitigate the heaviness of our wayward thinking by replenishing our thoughts with His thoughts.

Let's take a little step back to the first verse of Romans Chapter 12, where we see that this renewal process is not just for the mind. It is a head-to-toe restoration that calls for the believer to present their full bodies as a living sacrifice. This is the full scope of our reasonable service—to yield, to be holy, and to be acceptable unto God. The only way to accomplish this request is to begin by submitting our thoughts and ways to God. Why? Because we are not only His creation, but also the recipients of His goodness and His mercies as described in Romans chapters 1–11, including but not limited to His righteousness, justification, redemption, propitiation, patience, peace, reconciliation, grace, love, and kindness. Therefore, it is the least we can do in recognition of His care for us. Plus, yielding our minds and our all to Him is the safest thing to do. I will talk about this idea of being safe in an example coming up.

As described in Chapter Four of this book, a healthy demonstration of breaking bad is all about realigning our attitude to change our disposition. Staying focused is necessary when our goals are threatened or seem too far out of reach. Without proper focus, we run the risk of turning into someone we are not when pressures and disappointments are at an all-time high. Turning our thoughts over to God can help our focus and awareness. We will be able to concentrate again, and we will be able to expand our mindfulness to guard against operating in mental negativity again.

Let's visit the account of the first marital relationship in the Bible. Adam and Eve were kicked out of the Garden of Eden because of their disobedience. In what they thought was an opportunity to expand their understanding and awareness, they ate fruit from the Tree of Knowledge of Good and Evil because the serpent convinced Eve that God was withholding knowledge from them. This was not true. Although there were things that they did not know, God was, in fact, protecting them through this instruction.

To keep them alive and benefactors of all that the garden offered, God instructed Adam and Eve not to eat from the Tree of Knowledge of Good and Evil so that they would not use their free will to sin. If that were to happen and they later ate from the Tree of Life, in their sinful state, they would not have any opportunity for redemption or repentance. They would have stayed sinners and separated from God forever. Consequently, this is why they were ejected from the garden. Now that they were susceptible to this understanding, there was no more potential for them to govern themselves accordingly. They had already proven to be disobedient.

Being banished from the Garden of Eden as part of their curse ended their access to a beautiful environment that provided everything they needed, including safety, peace, and freedom. Eve mistakenly depended on the word of the serpent, and consequently, Adam mistakenly depended on the word of Eve. Their dependence on God's word was the furthest thing from their minds. It was as if they had no consideration for the instructions that were given to them by The One who had created them, provided for them, and loved them. There was no reasonable service on their part, despite the absolute evidence of God's mercy.

When we consider Adam and Eve's irreversible error, known as the Fall of Man, we can see how the Apostle Paul's tone and word choice in Romans Chapter 12 is so critical for our understanding and awareness. In verse 1, Paul "beseeches" believers to dedicate themselves to God. His strong desire summons our attention as readers. I might even argue that he begs for us to understand that since we are and have been walking in the mercies of God already, there is a continuous responsibility to submit ourselves fully back to Him and to each other in servanthood. The Apostle also uses the word "prove" in the second verse to highlight even more responsibility for us to scrutinize or examine our authentic service to God and demonstrate to the world that God is good. God's work is already proven to us by His mercies, and it will be proven again and again to the world as we engage God in this manner.

Can I just take the time to say, "Hallelujah"? Thank you. Hallelujah!

Of all the things that we can be doing or saying when situations do not go our way, we get the awesome opportunity to work with God to prove His honor as we allow Him to manage our bodies and our minds, ultimately for His honor and for Him to get the best out of us. The hope of our next breakthrough lies in this awareness.

Dear Reader, you can have a pathway leading to the decisions, knowledge, resources, understanding, and peace that is required for your specific situation. Trust God enough to allow Him to INTERRUPT your current thoughts about it. Release the reins and let Him in. Know, without a shadow of doubt, that He is there, and He has the answers you crave.

Let's take a closer look at the benefits of yielding our minds.

Decision making with God. We just glanced at Adam and Eve's fateful decision making after Eve's discussion with the serpent. Remember how the serpent's words influenced Eve and then Eve's words influenced Adam? Had the couple made an intentional effort to keep God's word a priority, it would not have been so easy for them to forget what was said.

This is how we act in modern times. We may study, but we are not studying to show ourselves approved. In 2 Timothy 2:15, we are taught that a laborer or worker studies their craftsmanship closely so that they are never ashamed of what they produce and to also demonstrate their ability to handle their tasks. As believers, we ought to approach God's word as a student: studying it closely to walk in it correctly, and to handle and interpret the truths thereof appropriately. It is easier to hear God's voice when we study what He has said. When we have studied what He has said, it is easier to know what He prefers for us to do. Our choices become His choices. Our steps become His steps.

Gaining knowledge with God. Similar to decision making, we must know what God's word says. We must study it and handle it with care. The gaining of new knowledge is achieved when we meditate on God's word and seek Him for deeper meanings. How many times have you come across a familiar scripture and realized that you have a greater perspective of it now than you did before? Nothing changed. The words are the same. But through study, meditation, and application our minds are renewed. The specific insight that we gain is reflective of the time spent absorbing and applying the word to our everyday life.

Revelation's knowledge of God's word comes to those who are ready to receive the deeper things of God, to include spiritual gifts, discernment, and specific opportunities to use those gifts. John, the author of the Book of Revelation, also known as the great Revelator, said that he "was in the Spirit on the Lord's day". This snippet of Revelation 1:10, describes not just one moment in John's life where he received the revelation of Jesus Christ to the world specifically through a handful of letters written to seven churches in Asia Minor. Those few words also represent a lifestyle where John would regularly position himself to hear, see, and experience more information and knowledge from God. Knowledge with such a priority that it would be referenced in those times, in our times now, and in the times to come.

Resources with God. Similar to gaining knowledge, positioning ourselves to encounter the deeper things of God will not only reveal powerful and pertinent information, but also powerful and pertinent gifts. God is a giving God, and He enjoys gifting us with tools to complete our assignments and to help one another. As mentioned in our review of Romans 12:1–2, there is a reasonable service expected of us as partakers of God's mercy. If we keep reading more of Romans Chapter 12, we can see His mercy and His grace working together. In verses 3–14, we will find a list of ministry gifts or gifts of grace, designed to sustain the church. These gifts build up the people of God and express God's love to others. Every believer has a gift or gifts to render. Your gift is a resource for completing your assignment. It is also a helpful resource to assist others as they strive to complete their assignments.

Understanding with God. It is my personal belief that when you know better, you do better. Knowing God better will provide this same kind of result—doing better! This year the vision for my church is "Trust You More" and the scriptural reference is Proverbs 3:5, which reads, "Trust in the LORD with all thine heart, and lean not unto thine own understanding." If we want more from God, there is more to do. While God has always made himself available to us, we have to do what is necessary to experience His availability.

Getting closer to Him pays off tremendously. Anyone you spend a significant amount of time with is thereby better acquainted with you. Although He knows all about us, we do not know enough of Him. If we want to experience more of God, we must bridge the gap between our desire for God's presence and His omnipresence, with daily awareness of His presence through trust. When we "trust in the Lord with all thine heart" we learn how to yield (there's that word again—YIELD!).

How do we do this? Looking at the definition for the word yield, we know that it means to produce or provide, to give way to pressure or influence. Therefore, we must acknowledge and give way to the pressure and influence of God, which is far above and beyond our own abilities or current situation. When we "lean not to thine own understanding," we must become teachable. Therefore, we practice posturing ourselves towards God and not towards ourselves or anyone else. The way we see things is not always the way it really is. By trading our understanding for God's, we invoke trust and rely on His ways more and more. After all, God's thoughts are not our thoughts, neither are His ways our ways (Isaiah 55:8).

Peace with God. Isn't peace what we ultimately want when our thoughts are restless and getting through a break seems unattainable? Gaining an understanding of God through trust is the pathway to peace. I challenge you to reflect on a stormy time in your past and determine whether or not a greater level of peace would have been helpful, despite the circumstance or outcome. What if your loved one died too soon? Nothing would be greater than to have more time with them. But if you could just get some peace about their absence—not necessarily acceptance—perhaps you could forge ahead each day without them a little better. Having peace, in this example, is not asking you to be in agreement with their death (acceptance) but reconciling that it has happened and there is no undoing it—that's peace.

As believers, we trust that we will see our believing loved ones in heaven, and experience God's promised paradise together. Yet, we also struggle to gain peace at death. Therefore, we strive to obtain what Philippians 4:7 teaches: "the peace of God, which passeth all understanding". This is to say that peace with God goes beyond anything we can understand on our own. The previous verse helps us to get there when it says, "Be careful for nothing; but in every thing by prayer and supplication with thanksgiving let your requests be made known unto God" (Philippians 4:6).

Through prayer and great seeking, the kind of peace that is required when nothing will soothe us or quench our desperation as we languish, can still be achieved and experienced. It may still hurt, but you can make it through one day at a time. You will look up one day and still wonder how is it that your loved one is no longer with you, but you can breathe better through the flood of memories and tears, and continue carrying them in your heart.

Are you aware that when we experience happy and joyful times, our thoughts should be on God? Are you aware, that when we experience difficult times, our thoughts should STILL be on God? Go back to the prayer you wrote at the beginning of this chapter. Add to it, as you see fit. Make a request for God to add to you the awareness of His presence throughout the ups and downs of life. Then take some time to meditate on the scriptures listed at the end of this chapter. Let them help you streamline your thoughts. Then finally, practice setting aside a portion of your daily prayer time for meditation. Let God interrupt and penetrate your mind and let Him navigate your thoughts for a greater breakthrough.

Meditation Scriptures: Romans 12:1–2, 2 Timothy 2:15, Proverbs 3:5, Isaiah 55:8, Philippians 4:6–7, Isaiah 26:3, Proverbs 4:23, Jeremiah 33:3, Proverbs 16:3.

Chapter 7:
Breaking Forward

ACTION!

Some breaks in life leave you with no choice but to move. These breaks spark an immediate change or action. Despite their level of difficulty, breaks can operate as a stimulant, forcing you to respond or move forward. How you respond is up to you.

Other breaks in life will leave you where you are, without a push or a spark. Once you are dropped and broken by the magnitude of a situation, you might feel like neglected luggage. Unclaimed. Lost. Without purpose. Without vision. These feelings can cause stagnation and a strong resistance to any kind of action at all. How long you stay there is up to you.

I have learned that however we act or however long it takes us to act, it should not be left up to the force of the break to decide. Let's not give the break more power than it already has. The decision to move should be ours. I may get the wind knocked out of me, but that does not have to mean I never breathe again! Besides, I like breathing and being broken should never change that. What am I saying here? Experiencing a break can add to me or take away from me, but it cannot stop me.

So, what is your usual course of action? Do you get moving towards your healing and recovery? Or do you sit in your sorrow and take up residence in your broken place? I want you to know that hope for a breakthrough is already embedded in you. Our hope is activated when our decision making is intentional, because not moving forward is actually deciding to remain still. When it comes to our recovery, if we have yet to decide to do what is healthy, we have, in fact, decided to do what is not the healthiest. A delayed response is still a response. So, you have a choice in the matter, even when you think you do not.

Without a doubt, grief, pain, and healing take time. In these cases, there should be no rush to act, except to posture ourselves towards recovery. In previous chapters, we have seen a few scenarios where recovery was the only urgent primary action.

Remember the woman in the car accident from Chapter One? Instantly, her life changed due to the icy conditions of an evening drive. Because she was still alive, every action taken was to gain a better quality of life despite the severity of her condition. There was no other action to take. No sitting still. No waiting.

Remember Rose in Chapter Five? She struggled with the physical, emotional, and psychological effects of aging. Not to mention her grief after the death of her husband of fifty years. This was followed by a scary encounter with Sharon, who could have killed her when she drugged her to gain access to her credit cards and bank account. Initially, Rose wanted to fade into her sofa and drift off to a place in her mind where she could still be with her deceased husband. But she woke up and realized a greater purpose in her pain, which was to walk with others in their pain.

Rose would eventually become a physical representation of God's warmth during a cold time in someone else's life. This, along with the example of how we deal with death and grief presented at the end of Chapter Six, is how we realize that it is during our darkest struggles that we become aware of God's presence and His peace.

All of these are examples where an unlimited amount of time is needed, and the amount of time used is different for everyone. Still, the necessary action is deciding to take the time to get through it. Movement is still required. Can you move through your grief? Yes, you can. You can breathe through it. You can journal through it. You can get counseling or therapy to help you through it. Exercise through it. Spend time with family and friends to get through it. Move and get through it. There is no rush to get through it and there is no push to get out of it. Remember the difference between getting through something and getting out of something from Chapter One? I do not ever recommend getting out of grief or going through grief quickly. But go through it and do it at your own pace.

There are other examples of how to take action, like my own personal scenario in Chapter Three. My struggle with anger revealed that it can certainly push you towards a negative physiological response. But anger can also wake you up like a call to action and cause you to move in a way that will invoke a positive change. My initial response was not positive. But my vow to re-purpose the passion in my anger was a positive one that I have remained committed to ever since.

In Chapter Four, Brady had a breaking bad moment on the school bus and revealed a side of himself that he nor anyone else knew existed. Which persona was the real Brady? Within the span of a week, Sara Jane experienced two different versions of Brady. Although she was falling for the first, it was the second who pushed her away.

What about the example of the young executive in Chapter One who experienced a break due to stress and anxiety? He grew up quickly when his family had an immediate hardship and home life as he knew it was turned upside down. He developed a way of managing emergencies and various urgent matters by exhibiting strength, maturity, and dependability for those he cared about and for those who needed it. But there was no rock for him to lean on, only the load of more fast paced urgent needs as a reward. He never acted for himself. So, his body made the decision for him.

Then there is our discussion about rejection in Chapter Two. Learning that we do not have enough to satisfy a new opportunity, or we do not have enough to satisfy the needs of a relationship can sting and stagnate. If we are not careful, an experience with rejection can disqualify all our other gifts, skills, talents, and wisdom—

if we let it. DO NOT LET IT! It may sting, but you can heal. It may stagnate you for the moment, but you can move. You do not have to live on rejection island.

These last few examples demonstrate that an immediate course of action was taken, but not for the better. Please remember that the choice is yours. Again, how you move or act and how long it takes you to move or act is up to you!

The hope for our next break through is that there is still life to experience. Yes, there are more breaks to break through, but there are also more bridges to cross and more beauty to behold.

One scripture that I like to offer about movement and action talks about how our actions are rooted in God. Read it out loud:

> *"That they should seek the Lord, if haply they might feel after him, and find him, though he be not far from every one of us:*
>
> *For in him we live, and move, and have our being; as certain also of your own poets have said, For we are also his offspring."*
> *(Acts 17:27-28, KJV)*

With this brief snippet of the Sermon on Mars Hill found in Acts 17:27–28, the Apostle Paul preaches to heathens who worshiped false gods and were without the true God in the world. This message was intended to introduce them and the Jews to Jesus, as the Redeemer, using prophecies and miracles. Paul wanted to penetrate their worldly habits of superstitions and idol worship with the understanding that the true God was alive and not dead like their idols.

The One who gave them life is full of life and was neither crafted by the hands of men nor limited to dwell in objects and temples made by men. This living, breathing God was available and near to anyone who sought Him and reached out to Him. How can this be? Because He is life and life dwells in Him. Therefore, being in relationship with Him gives us access to Him and in Him is the very essence of our lives, our movement, and our existence. Again, what does this mean? It means that no matter what happens around us or to us, there is nothing else responsible or powerful enough to help us manage this life besides The One who gave us life. Under His management, there is more life, more movement, and more purpose beyond every stagnating situation. Hallelujah!

This scripture is a necessity for the times that we live in because we need to be reminded of just how close we are and can be to God. You can build your idols, but there is no life or movement there. You can build your temples, but they are not big enough for the divine presence of God. But this life that God has given us—THAT is where He desires to live. He desires to LIVE inside of us, MOVE us, and EXIST through us.

Dear Reader, you must MOVE!

I had the pleasure of spending a weekend with the awesome women of St. Paul Church of God in Christ, in Emporia, Virginia, in September 2021, where my friend, Rev. Brandon C. Allen is the pastor. As the guest facilitator, I shared with them the importance of movement at their women's conference.

Movement is an act of changing a physical location or position, or an act of having these things changed. Movement is an expression of change. Movement indicates development. Unlike the heathens who were the audience for Paul's sermon mentioned earlier, our hope is not, and cannot be, placed in anything that does not cause us to move, change, or develop. In the worst of times, action is needed for healing and recovery. In the best of times, action is needed to continue our journey towards wholeness and balance.

Dear Reader, you must MOVE!

I am hoping, in the face of your current or next break, that you experience spiritual movement, physical movement, emotional movement, and relational movement.

Spiritual Movement is developing your spiritual armor in God. This includes spiritual disciplines such as meditating, praying, fasting, and studying. Richard Foster, the author of Celebration of Discipline, declares that God intended the disciplines of spiritual life to be for ordinary people, not just for scholars or those specifically called to a life of intercession. He further clarifies that these disciplines are "best exercised in the midst of our relationships." This highlights the kind of commitment it takes for a believer to explore their own inner life and indicates that this exploration will not only benefit the believer, but also those around them. Therefore, any believer, despite their calling or role in organized ministry, has the responsibility to pray, fast, study, and meditate to nurture their relationship with God and also to practice these things in their various communities and with others in their communities.

Physical Movement is developing your physical stamina in God. Is your daily posture rooted in prayer? Can you sustain that posture? We want strength, but we must fuel up! We are reminded in 3 John 1:2 that while tending to the salvation of our souls, we should also seek to be in good health. That scripture reads, "Beloved, I wish above all things that thou mayest prosper and be in good health, even as thy soul prospereth." Doing God's work requires spiritual focus and a quality of life that affords us the appropriate fitness for the work.

With intense prayer, prayer along with fasting, or the kind of targeted prayer that you observe during intercession, it is not good enough to just schedule the time or take the time, we must be ready to take on the posture as well (kneeling, lying prostrate on the floor, walking, prolonged standing). Then there are other physical aspects of servanthood, including tending to the needs of the sick and shut in, visitations, food deliveries, and the many meetings to coordinate it all. The physical part of servanthood requires good nutrition, exercise, regular doctor's visits, good hygiene, and proper sleep.

I'll talk more about Coach Landry in the next chapter, but he understands how to get the best out of people, even when the process is difficult. Keeping up with our physical health can be an overwhelming task, but it is necessary for servanthood. The woman in the icy car accident from Chapter One was used to being physically active in her daily routine. But after the accident, she and her family could have benefited from those who were willing to be their arms and legs while she recovered (picking up prescriptions, getting groceries, babysitting, pet-sitting, household chores, and transportation).

Emotional Movement is developing your coping skills in God. Becoming aware of and developing our emotional intelligence includes self-awareness (ensuring that our actions and thoughts reflect our core beliefs), self-management (how we handle stress, spend our time, and exercise problem-solving skills), and social awareness (being open and understanding towards others whose cultures, backgrounds, and behaviors are not our own). Identifying and understanding these things about ourselves helps us to manage our emotions effectively, especially in difficult situations. Developing these skills in God, means that we look to biblical principles for alignment and guidance in these areas and for help when we are out of balance. Being in tune with ourselves to this extent could have helped Brady, in Chapter Four, avoid an uncharacteristic outburst that eclipsed his true character for years afterwards.

Relational Movement is investing in your relationship with God and nurturing a healthier perspective of your relationship with others. In We Collide, I referenced the symbolism of the cross as a way to define, grow, and repair our relationship with God (vertically), and our relationships with each other (horizontally). The vertical pathway is intersected with the horizontal pathway, indicating that when one relationship has experienced a breach, the other relationship suffers as well. We must be conscientious of our actions along each path. What we nurture or fail to nurture has bidirectional consequences. So, if there is a break in one of your horizontal relationships, it does not have to negatively affect your other relationships. Instead, allow your healthier relationships to sustain you while you recover and heal. And, please let your vertical relationship with God be a foundational power source for every relationship you engage in.

These four movements require intentional pursuit. The kind of movement that prevents debilitation and immobilization. You can move now, or you can move later, but make it your goal to move forward no matter what.

You can act now and turn to the next chapter, where we will learn more about these movements through application.

CHAPTER 8:
BREAKING GROUND

APPLICATION!

Many times, we know what to do or we agree with what we are told to do. Yet, we still fail to follow through. I have said many times that life will try its best to break us. The reality is that we will break down sometimes. Still, there is hope.

We need to believe that we can make it, by courageously looking forward. We need new information and knowledge that only transforms into wisdom for our everyday lives after we appropriately utilize what we have learned. We need new tools and methods in our possession that we actually learn how to use. We need support from each other that goes beyond the first few minutes of our break. Essentially, with hope, knowledge, tools, and support during our breaking experience, we can make it to the other side of any break. This chapter will help us break ground and follow through.

Chapter Seven nicely summarized the many ways that our paths diverge when we experience a break. Since getting through our struggles includes, but is not limited to, addressing **accidents, acceptance, anger, attitude, aging,** and **awareness**, forward action must take place. This forward **action** begins now with the **application** of a unique journaling experience.

Oh, how I wish I could have seen your face as you read that last sentence about a unique journaling experience coming up. Are you open to it, or did you reject the notion right away? Do not be like most people who ask, "Where do I go from here?", "How do I get started?", or "What's next?", and never commit to doing the work that takes you to the next place. Do not be like most people who are given an assignment that will aid them along their journey, but then turn their nose up at the assignment.

Tom Landry, one of the most innovative coaches in the National Football League and former coach of the Dallas Cowboys, defined coaching as "making men do what they don't want, so they can become what they want to be." Even twenty-two years after his death, Coach Landry is ranked number eight on the list of "25 Greatest Head Coaches in NFL History", according to Aaron Tallent, in his Athlon Sports article (last updated Feb 18, 2022).

Coach Landry knew how to get the best out of his players and we can learn from both his impactful statement and his historical record. Sometimes, we must do what we do not want to do in order to get to the places we know we want to be.

Hard work gets the work done and it is time for you to put the work in for YOU! So, please allow me to coach you through this chapter.

Let's begin by dealing with our tendency for stagnation. Stagnation means lack of activity, growth, or development. What is holding you down or holding you back so that you cannot move? Is it fear? Is it a lack of resources? Take a minute to think about it and list your reasons here.

***What is holding you back from doing work on yourself?
List all the reasons why you are stagnant or
afraid to move:***

_____

_____

_____

_____

_____

JOURNAL

Let's get specific. List all the people or things that are currently keeping you from focusing on yourself right now:

_____

_____

_____

_____

_____

_____

_____

_____

_____

_____

_____

_____

_____

_____

_____

_____

_____

_____

Declare right now that you will make it a priority to work on yourself. Declare that you will overcome your compulsions, laziness, toxic beliefs, and toxic people in your life so that you can focus on yourself. Write your declaration here.

I, _____, declare on this day, _____, that I will:

_____

_____

_____

_____

_____

_____

_____

_____

_____

_____

_____

_____

You will need strength to face your fears and to release yourself from toxicity and compulsions. I am praying for your strength. Read through the prayers that I have strategically written to help you overcome the struggles that often overtake us when we experience a break. Let's pray together.

Are you struggling with accidents? Let's pray:

Father, You are holy and just, and I thank You for Your listening ear. I know You see everything and You are aware of everything concerning me. Thank You for Your omniscience.

In this prayer, I seek Your comfort and Your strength as I work to recover from accidental damage. I know there is no full recovery apart from having a relationship with You. So, I dedicate myself to spiritual and physical healing.

It is my desire to be in Your care because there is no one else who can provide the wholeness that I need. Lord, heal my hurt and heal those who hurt me, whether intentional or not. Show me how to move forward without ill will, spite, or retaliation of any kind towards those who have afflicted me. Help me to forgive as I too stand in need of Your forgiveness. I want to reflect Your light, even though this road to recovery has been slow and long. I want to reflect Your grace and mercy. You have been more than generous with Your great benefits, and I want to share them with others.

I know I do not deserve it, neither can I earn it, but for every accident, Lord, show me how to make it through. This is my prayer, in Jesus' matchless name.

Amen.

Are you struggling with acceptance? Let's pray:

Father, there is no other love like Your unconditional love, and I thank You for the way You love me. You have accepted me as I am and continue to shape me to be more. Thank You for Your compassion.

I speak Your word over my life concerning who I am. I know that I am fearfully and wonderfully made. Help me to know it deep in my soul, without a doubt. Keep the negative whispers out of my ears, I want to hear Your voice more. Keep the shadowy reflections from my mirror. I want to see more of You in me and less of the world. As I learn to trade my doubt for Your truth, please strengthen me with Your right hand, especially in the face of rejection.

Lord, help me not to fall under the weight of depression, isolation, anxiety, and distress. As I draw closer to You, let confidence be my portion. You are my blessed assurance now and forever. I will call upon Your name in my darkest hour and I will praise Your name through every challenge.

Thank You for creating me in Your image. Thank You for giving me life and for the opportunity to live it more abundantly. In Jesus' name, I pray.

Amen.

Are you struggling with anger? Let's pray:

Father, You are gentle and kind. You are also stern and strong. You sent Your Son to be both the Lion and the Lamb to protect us from the destruction of our sins. I thank You for the balance of Your ways.

I seek your balance as I learn to express myself more appropriately. Your word says to be angry and sin not. Teach me how to communicate my needs and demonstrate my emotions with clarity and without fault. Help me not to harm or cause harm to others just to prove a point, to gain leverage, or out of frustration.

Jesus is described as meek and mild, and I know there is no weakness in Him. Help me to portray strength in a non-abusive way. Help me with my reactions when I have been hurt or abused. Keep me from repeating the cycle. Aid me, oh God, as I help those who are less fortunate. Help me to protect them and my family in an honorable way.

No matter the situation, I want the world to see more of You and less of me. I pray, in Jesus' name.

Amen.

Are you struggling with anger? Let's pray:

My Father, I honor You, for Your thoughts are not my thoughts and Your ways are not my ways. Thank You for Your Holiness.

I declare that I have the mind of Christ. Help me to think more like You every day. When my thoughts and intentions fall beneath Your expectations, remind me that You have raised up a standard by which I am to be guided. Help me to see myself and others through Your lens. Help me to handle every challenge with godly character.

I no longer desire to carry the weight or the curse of anger. I no longer want anger to be my default disposition. Heal my attitude. Manage the emotions of my heart. Manage my frustrations. Manage my tolerance. Grant me patience, wisdom, and a renewed focus.

Lord, I know that the weapons of my warfare are not carnal. I will turn to You as You fight my every battle. Thank You for the victory. In Jesus' mighty name.

Amen.

Are you struggling with aging? Let's pray:

My Father, You are Alpha and Omega, the Beginning and the End. I am so grateful that You hold all of our times in Your capable hands.

I thank You for my life, health, and strength. I thank You especially for the duration of my life because Your word says with long life You will satisfy me. I know there is a place for me in Your Promised Land after this life is over. But while I am still here, please grant me favor as I age.

Thank You in advance for good health, protection, physical and mental stamina, and a quality of life that is not only satisfying but conducive to my continued service to You and others. I want to be useful and valuable for the remainder of my days. Continue sharpening my gifts and help me to be ready when I am needed. Protect me when I am vulnerable and weak.

You are the Potter and I am the clay. Oh God, make me over and over as You see fit. In Jesus' name, I pray.

Amen.

Are you struggling with awareness? Let's pray:

My Father, Your word says that You are mindful of me. Who am I to be thought of the way You do? Help me to be more mindful of You.

I acknowledge that You are not only my foundation but also my sustenance. I look to You for power and the renewing of my mind. Knowledge is no good except I have knowledge of You. As I seek to know You more, show me the revelation of Your word. Increase my faith, understanding, and discernment. Minimize the confusion and make my pathways clear.

I know You own the cattle on a thousand hills, help me to be resourceful in You. I need the peace of knowing that my everything is wrapped up in You. As You enlarge my territory, I want to walk upright in your ways.

Amen.

JOURNAL

What is your personal prayer? Write it here:

_____

_____

_____

_____

_____

_____

_____

_____

_____

_____

_____

_____

_____

_____

Now, let's lend ourselves to moving spiritually, physically, emotionally, and relationally. This process will help you capture your own personal thoughts, set goals, and establish accountability for whatever is next for you despite any break you may have encountered, or the damage left in its wake.

Keep an open mind as you engage these next few pages. This journal is the beginning of a new journey towards freedom. You will experience relief as you identify unnecessary weights and decide to move beyond the difficult experiences. You will realize new strengths as you reconcile letting go of the past for the hope of the future.

Be honest with yourself through the change. Be intentional about getting your healing. There is work to do and you must be committed to doing the work of breaking through!

YOUR SPIRITUAL MOVEMENT: Currently, how often do you do the following in a week? Pray: _____, Study: _____, Meditate: _____. Over the next week, commit to developing your spiritual armor with a routine of prayer, study, and meditation. For each spiritual discipline, there is a set goal for each day. Write your time (in minutes) in the blank spaces. Push yourself to reach each daily goal.

	SUN	MON	TUE	WED	THU	FRI	SAT
Prayer Goal	5	5	5	10	10	15	15
Your Prayer Time							
Study Goal	10	10	15	15	20	25	30
Your Study Time							
Meditation Goal	5	5	5	10	10	15	15
Your Meditation Time							

When you pray, thank God for His goodness, ask for forgiveness, and help for you and others. Your prayer is a personal conversation with your Heavenly Father. When you study, search for scriptures or themes in scripture that interest you. Read them slowly for understanding. When you meditate, focus on something you've learned or a new characteristic you've discovered about God. Before you know it, you will have spent an hour a day before the Lord.

YOUR PHYSICAL MOVEMENT: Review the contributions you make to your overall health and wellness by observing your habits for a week. Which sentence describes your eating habits?

- I eat when I am happy, sad, or stressed. (Emotional Eater)
- If I see it, I eat it. (Unconscious Eater)
- I have an eating routine, I sometimes binge. (Habitual Eater)
- I am aware of everything I eat. (Critical Eater)
- I enjoy new foods and hardly watch portions. (Sensual Eater)
- I eat healthy foods and burn them off. (Energy Eater)

Despite your choice above, every option needs balance. We must learn to eat for fuel (energy), not for fun (celebration), and not while in a fog (mindlessness or disappointment). Adopt a healthier, balanced diet, minimize mindless snacking, and increase water intake.

Now, how would you describe your exercise habits? Circle the most accurate statement: "I exercise regularly", "I exercise once in a while", "Each time I start exercising, I fall off", "I never exercise". You must acknowledge where you are now and commit to being in a better place within a determined amount of time.

Make a commitment to enhance and achieve balance with your physical activity. Rewrite your poor habits from this week with intentional choices. Develop the discipline to recover your personal agency. As we continue to deal with the breaks of life, we must be certain that we are not the ones causing more stress or danger by ignoring our personal agency. Regain your power.

YOUR EMOTIONAL MOVEMENT: Let's work on our emotional intelligence by building up our self-awareness (core beliefs), self-management, and social awareness. This will help us to understand ourselves more and better manage our responses and actions through difficulty.

Your core beliefs are what you value most. Rate the following words from 1 (least meaningful) to 10 (most meaningful):

VALUE	RATE	VALUE	RATE	VALUE	RATE
Loyalty		Responsibility		Leadership	
Respect		Service		Relationships	
Honor		Integrity		Courage	
Love		Kindness		Trust	
Balance		Beauty		Achievement	
Faith		Creativity		Security	
Influence		Justice		Peace	
Knowledge		Optimism		Compassion	
Success		Community		Citizenship	
Adventure		Work Ethic		Growth	

Now, look at your ratings and circle the ten with the highest rating. These are your core values. While there are so many more words that could have been included in the list and so many different exercises to help you identify what is important, this is a good start to knowing more about yourself.

These are the things that mean the most to you in any situation at any given time. When everything is great and in the middle of adversity, these are the core values that you will either fight for or protect the most. These are also the values that you will be the most determined to display in your reaction and responses. Typically, the way you respond in difficult times is based on what you value the most.

Do not discard the remainder of the list. Perhaps there are some values that should be elevated to the top ten. As we grow, our values may change. A true test is to ask your closest family members and friends how they would rate you for each word. Then you will know if you actually demonstrate what you say you value the most.

Now, go back to the list and identify the things you value the most in others. Choose ten and write them here:

_____   _____

_____   _____

_____   _____

_____   _____

_____   _____

Are they the same as the things you value most for yourself? Note the similarities as well as the differences. Would you say that your expectation of yourself is greater or less than what you expect from others? Do you know why that is? Maybe there is no way to reconcile the difference right now, but keep it in mind and remember that the standard you have set for yourself may not be met by others, but it does not mean that they themselves do

not have standards and core values that are important to them.

Some of our stress and time management can be addressed in our physical and spiritual movements. But we need to spend our time wisely by developing tools for stress relief and for problem solving. The next time you find yourself tensing up when faced with a challenge or demand, try one or more of the following:

- Tapping: Repeatedly tap certain areas of your body to realign your focus and decrease the intensity of the moment. Those areas include: the fat part of your palm below the thumb, temples, forehead, nose, chin, inside the elbow, knees, and ears.

- Counting: Count from 1 to 25, then back down to 1 repeatedly.

- Music Favorite: Listen to the music of your choice for 15 minutes.

- Music Alternative: Listen to a different genre than what you usually listen to for 15 minutes. Choose a theme or song title based on what you are dealing with at the moment.

- Meditate/Pray/Study: Implement what you have learned from the spiritual movement.

- Breathing One: Take deep breaths in and exhale slowly for one full minute. Repeat for a total of 3 minutes.

- Breathing Two: Take a deep breath and hold for 15 seconds, then exhale slowly. Repeat for a total of 3 minutes.

The next time you are faced with a dilemma that calls for an important decision, try my "4i Decision Making Tool". This tool will help you feel more confident about the decision you make and ensure that you are methodical as you consider the many possibilities.

The 4i Decision Making Tool
(Inform, Investigate, Instead, Implement)

INFORM: Get your resources together, identify current trends, study the market, and be aware of the extent of your own skills and experience. Get advice from others who are more knowledgeable in that particular field.

INVESTIGATE: Take the time to find out about the risks of each possibility while learning about the benefits. You need to know costs, how much time is needed, and the level of effort. You also need to know what perks are provided as well. Then when you look at the risks alongside the benefits, you can better determine if the benefits are actually WORTH the risks. This is your analysis. Making a decision is not just saying "YES" or "NO" to an opportunity. It is an agreement to all the fine print.

INSTEAD: Sometimes we only initially explore what seems to be the obvious options. We are creatures of habit, and even with a new decision we can be robotic, choosing what is familiar. Our investigation may turn up alternative paths to achieve the same goal. In other words, keep your options open. Do not be afraid to try something new and unconventional. ALSO, we should step back and ask ourselves what would happen if we did not make this decision at all. What will happen instead, if we do not decide? What will happen if we let this decision slip away? Will things stay the same or will we have to be responsible for an option we did not want or choose? Do not be so casual about the process that you do not choose at all!

IMPLEMENT: It is time to decide. But just before we do, let's organize what we have learned. Organization is the key to seeing the big picture. Seeing the big picture helps you to plot where you are and where you would like to go. For each potential possibility (decision), make a short list of what you have learned and HOW you will pursue that decision (next steps). It will look like this:

1. Decision A
    a. Information
    b. Benefits/Risks
    c. Next steps
2. Decision B
    a. Information
    b. Benefits/Risks
    c. Next steps

Consider each decision's short list. Which speaks to you the most? Which one seems like a better option overall?

In summary, INFORM yourself by gathering enough information. INVESTIGATE all the risks and benefits. INSTEAD of what you usually do, or INSTEAD of deciding at all, what will happen? IMPLEMENT your plan after outlining a short list for each option and making your decision.

Now, onto social awareness, which is being open and understanding towards others whose cultures, backgrounds, and behaviors are not our own. You can broaden your perspective through your relationship movement, but here are some questions to consider:

- How diverse is your core group of friends?
- List the different genres of music you enjoy.
- Of your favorite foods, how many nationalities are represented?
- Of all the people who are in your regular workspaces or living spaces, do you ever engage the ones who do not look like you? If not, why not?
- When traveling, do you engage in the culture of that location (food, art, history), or do you stay close to the common tourist sites?
- Do you ever go out of your way to make others who are different, feel comfortable in your presence?

YOUR RELATIONAL MOVEMENT: Developing and maintaining relationships is very important. You are not alone, despite your circumstances and how you may be feeling. Others in the world have experienced similar (and often worse) experiences. We need each other not just for companionship and love, but also for understanding and compassion, especially when we encounter the breaks of life. This is where our hope comes from. Let's look at the relationships we have.

1. Make a list of all your close relationships. Which ones would you define as your top five?

2. List all the communities you are part of. Which ones would you define as your top five?

3. How many new relationships did you gain in the past two years?

4. How many of these new relationships made your top five relationships list? Name them.

5. How many new communities did you gain in the past two years?

6. How many of these new communities made your top ten communities list? Name them.

7. How do you nurture the relationships in your life?

8. What contributions have you made to the communities you belong to?

9. Are you satisfied with your relationships and communities?

10. Have you considered whether or not your relationships and communities are satisfied with your presence and contributions?

Finally, choose an accountability partner. You will share your goals and progress with this person and allow them to check in with you from time to time to see how things are going. List the names of at least three people who you are willing to share this journey with:

_____, _____, _____.

Come back to this chapter as often as you need to. Come back to be reminded how to take action and break ground before, during, or after any break. Come back to review where you were when you first completed this task. Come back to compare where you are now, concerning the specifics of the break you were experiencing at the time. Come back to this chapter to keep your testimony fresh in your heart and mind.

Returning to this chapter will also free your mind as you explore other options for breaking ground and recovering after a break. Praying and journaling is a big help. But also meditation will keep you mindful, yoga will keep you centered, and breathing exercises will calm you. Other suggestions may include healthy eating, making time for friends, making time for your hobbies, or discovering new ones.

Come back to remind yourself that the breaks of life do not have to break you! Now, use this last page to monitor where you are, where you are going, and the time it takes to get there. The commitment date is the day you begin your journey. In each of the movement blocks below, summarize how you started, your progress, and the end result. Note the date of completion and celebrate your breakthrough.

COMMITMENT DATE	SPIRITUAL MOVEMENT	PHYSICAL MOVEMENT	EMOTIONAL MOVEMENT	RELATIONAL MOVEMENT	COMPLETION DATE

CHAPTER 9:
BREAKING THROUGH, TOGETHER

ALL IN!

Every breakthrough win for an individual is one more breakthrough win, collectively. A celebration should be planned, and a bell should ring for the world to hear as a sign that breakthroughs are possible, despite the severity of any situation. Also worthy of celebration is knowing that there are more wins for everyone and more hope for the kinds of breaks that are the most difficult. If you are concerned about the increase of collective wins, then you are "ALL IN"!

When you break through, others do too and when breaking through for others becomes your concern, then that is what I call being "ALL IN". So, what if we were "all in"? How can we celebrate the breakthroughs of others and how can we help each other to have more breakthroughs? Let's find out how.

To celebrate these individual wins more, the individual must learn to let others in, when appropriate. We must be mindful that it is okay to let the ones who have demonstrated their love and concern for us into our closed spaces. We have boundaries for a reason—to protect and shield ourselves from negative people and experiences. But there comes a time when we must open those boundaries to get the help that we need.

God created us individually, but He created us to exist collectively. Respectfully, we must remember that the ones we have let into our personal space to help us have boundaries too. Therefore, we must utilize the help and not abuse it. The best way to have trust and create balance with those who help us in our breaking moments is to choose people and coordinate the necessary lifelines when we are in a healthy place. Choosing a lifeline when we are in the middle of a break can be stressful, and we may not choose well under duress.

We must allow ourselves to be celebrated. Going through hard times is tough. Coming out on the other side is worthy of recognition. Be mindful that small wins can be just as hard to come by as big wins, so every step towards any win is worth celebrating. Also, we must remember to be helpful when we are healthy and strong again. Lend a hand, be someone's lifeline, assist, and mostly love on others when they are breaking.

To celebrate individual wins more, we must be our authentic selves when others let us into their personal spaces. They do not need us to solve all their problems, or any problem for that matter. You do not have to have any answers, just lend your presence and your time. Walk with them along their journey. Do not make any promises, but know what you are capable of, and keep your word. Celebrate their small wins as much as their big wins.

To celebrate these collective wins more, we should shift the culture within community. What if we were concerned about breaking through with each other more than breaking down one another? There would be less gossiping, and fewer instances of bullying, especially bullying on social media platforms. There would be less anxiety when it came to being in community because there would be fewer personal attacks when we disagree and less need to be on guard due to our differences.

That's not all we should do. We should identify similarities and unique traits more often than isolating. Going through tough times can be difficult, but if we acknowledge similar difficulties while remembering that we respond to the same set of circumstances differently, then we can provide more space for more wins. The alternative is insisting that every win looks and feels the same for everybody. That is unreasonable and counterproductive.

We also need to capitalize on every breakthrough and build winning momentum. What can the momentum of multiple breakthroughs do? It can sprinkle hope in dark places. Instead of being angry about our current difficult experiences and refusing to have hope for change because change seems so far away, we can show each other that change, relief, peace, and wholeness are not too far out of reach. Collective wins make hope accessible to more individuals, even in the darkest of times. It is not enough for one or two to have hope. The more we have hope and become that hope for others, the more can be accomplished.

As mentioned in Chapter Six, being one body in Christ causes us to work together as members of one another. Working together is just the beginning. For as much as we labor together, we also endure, grow, win, and overcome together too. Please keep this in mind as we all experience the kinds of breaks that make us want to give up. Not just give up hope. Sometimes we give up on everything. What if each laborer continued the labor, without taking their hand off the plow or looking back? Luke 9:62 teaches us that, "No man, having put his hand to the plough, and looking back, is fit for the kingdom of God." When we are there for each other, when we have chosen our lifelines, when we make room for others to help in our time of need, we can reassure one another that there is more, despite this difficult time of our lives. We can be laborers of hope, encouragement, wisdom, and healing.

What if we were our brother's keeper—keeping each other as we continue the work? How do we make this happen? What would this look like? In Genesis 4:9, we see what it does not look like in a conversation between God and Cain. "And the LORD said unto Cain, Where is Abel thy brother? And he said, I know not: Am I my brother's keeper?"

Cain was not his brother's keeper. His response was sarcastically pessimistic, showing no regard or genuine concern for his brother. He had just killed him, and he did not care. Other biblical translations show Cain's mockery using phrases like, "Am I my brother's guardian?" (NLT), "Is it my job to take care of my brother?" (NCV), "Am I supposed to take care of my brother?" (GNT), and

"Am I his babysitter?" (MSG). The point here is that Cain dealt with his brother out of anger and jealousy while Cain was going through a break himself. This stemmed from seeing that the Lord had no respect for his offering, which was just some produce from the land he tilled, but great respect for Abel, who gave the first and the fattest calf from the cattle he raised.

I feel as though God's response was proving that if you cannot "keep" your brother, then you will learn what it means to also not be kept. He was cursed and banned from the earth, where his brother's blood spilled at his own hands. Because of the murder, Cain was destined to never yield any good crops and to forever wander the earth. Cain understood that under this curse, he could not produce, provide, or protect himself or his family. Yet, God did not allow Cain to become a target. Instead, He marked him so he would not be killed. God STILL KEPT Cain to the extent that He kept him alive to experience the curse, and to experience the magnitude of what he lost.

How can we be "all in" and keepers of our brother? Through prayer (a solemn request or expression of thanksgiving to God for our brother), support (to bear the weight of or to provide assistance for our brother), serving (to provide our brother with a product or service), covering (to provide shelter or protection for our brother, especially in danger), and loving (an intense feeling of deep affection towards our brother). Let's take a closer look at how to do this with the following scriptures and declarations.

Can You Pray For Your Brother?

- James 5:16: "Confess your faults one to another, and pray one for another, that ye may be healed. The effectual fervent prayer of a righteous man availeth much."
- When I pray for you, I will be as righteous as I can and I will pray fervently because I want you to be healed!

Can You Support Your Brother?

- Proverbs 27:17: "Iron sharpeneth iron; so a man sharpeneth the countenance of his friend."
- I will support/add to you because I want you to be your best. In fact, I will make an effort to do better each day so you can be better sharpened by me when we "rub". I want to "rub" you righteously, not the way that the world rubs you.

Can You Serve Your Brother?

- 1 Peter 4:10: "As every man hath received the gift, even so minister the same one to another, as good stewards of the manifold grace of God."
- In an act of service, I use my gifts (the good things that God gave me) to minister to you, because I want you to be whole and have everything that you need.

Can You Cover Your Brother?

- Proverbs 10:12: "Hatred stirreth up strifes: but love covereth all sins."
- If you should fall, I will help you and not expose you any further. Because of my affection towards you, I will aid you while you repent and recover.

Can You Love Your Brother?

- John 13:34: "A new commandment I give unto you, That ye love one another; as I have loved you, that ye also love one another."
- I will love you, because God has loved me, and He uses me to love you. I am a willing participant in God's love towards you.

With these scriptures and declarations, we can keep one another, labor with each other, and celebrate more wins in our community. At this point, we are not just "all in" for breakthrough wins, we are "all in" no matter what life brings our way.

The story of Cain and Abel not only teaches that being our brother's keeper is our responsibility, but also that we will be recognized for doing so. In Genesis 4:15, God is clear about Cain's discipline, "And the LORD set a mark upon Cain, lest any finding him should kill him." But in John 13:35, the Lord is also clear about the character of a disciple when He teaches that the identifying mark for everyone who is His disciple will be the way we love one another. If the church would carefully take this lesson to heart and always display true brotherly love towards each other, we would not ever have to worry about how we are perceived by the world. We are MARKED by how we treat each other.

When we are "all in", it means that we are aware of how we are "marked" and would prefer to be marked by our love and not by our hate or brokenness.

As we pursue our own individual and collective wins, as described in the previous chapter, I want to leave you with something that will keep you "all in". That is, focus on getting your breakthrough first and THEN you can help someone else get theirs. No matter what, keep your focus on becoming the healthiest you can be, before, during, and after each break, and in every way-mentally, physically, emotionally, and spiritually. Get your personal wins and the community will subsequently benefit in the process.

CHAPTER 10:
BREAKING CHAINS

ADVANCE!

Now that you have had your break, now that you have learned about the many divergent paths that can come from a break, the actions you can take towards your breakthrough, how to apply yourself for the best results, and what the implications of your breakthrough can be for the community, *WHAT NOW?* What do you do with this momentum? You know, the new thrust of energy that is pushing you forward. What do you do with the winds of victory blowing strong and fresh in your direction and in your favor? What do you do? Well...

You must advance! Take what used to be the broken pieces of a terrible experience and build something useful for the world to learn from and enjoy. Oftentimes, I come across people struggling to get to their breakthrough not just for the sole purpose of breaking through and becoming whole. Breaking through and becoming whole are certainly prioritized goals, but the achievement of such is not necessarily the end. When you turn around again after your breakthrough, and you are thriving once more, there is a purpose for that transformation.

Find your purpose or REVIVE your purpose and walk that path with new confidence. Is it okay to revive a purpose? Sure! We all change. What was right ten years ago, might not be now. What wasn't right then when we tried, does not mean it's not right now in this moment. Whether your purpose is revived or renewed, you are not meant to stay in the same position where you were when the break happened. Neither are you meant to stay in the same place where you received your breakthrough.

You must advance! Earlier, when I said to build something useful for the world to learn from and enjoy, that meant that you have the strength and the resolve and the tools now (not to mention the momentum) to grow not just despite your break, but because of it! Do not overload yourself with worry about what could have happened, what should have happened, or what did not happen. IT HAPPENED, and because of it, you learned something you would not have and you grew in areas you would not have. The momentum of your breakthrough should equip you with the wisdom of knowing that whatever it is you are about to do, whatever it is you are about to accomplish, was only made better because of the totality of what you have overcome. You must advance and do more because now you are so much more than what you used to be.

How many times have you seen people overcome a serious sickness but continue to indulge in the detrimental acts that led to their infirmity? People will get their healing, but will choose to remain unhealthy. They want to do the same things, eat the same things, or continue to do nothing more than what they have been doing, despite this new opportunity that has been given to them. Do not be like them. There is more for you. Do not waste the opportunity that your break and breakthrough have afforded you. The break was terrible, the breakthrough was terrific, and together, the break and the breakthrough are a transformational gift.

Uncover or revive the goals you set for yourself before the last break or before the last few breaks. Yes, go back as far as you need to go to get what you dropped when the breaks began to break you and distract you from your life's greatest aspiration. You have been released from all that broke you and all that tried to break you. You are free to retrieve only the things that are fitting for your new journey. You are no longer bound.

You must advance! The theme for my church in 2016 was "Focus & Push Beyond the Breakthrough". We were excited about that theme because it gave us hope for what could happen to us as we dealt with our various difficulties. It gave us hope beyond the victories that were realized during that time.

The corresponding theme scripture was Philippians 3:13–14, which reads, "Brethren, I count not myself to have apprehended: but this one thing I do, forgetting those things which are behind, and reaching forth unto those things which are before. I press towards the mark for the prize of the high calling of God in Christ Jesus."

The Apostle Paul writes to the Philippians confessing that although he is not all that he could be, he knows he is not what he used to be. He is committed to following and apprehending Christ because he has been apprehended by Him. In other words, Paul is compelled to keep on pressing to reach the end goal, which is "the high calling of God in Christ Jesus".

Now, Paul's "high calling" may not be your high calling. Whether it is or is not, there is still something GREATER to look forward to than all the things currently on your radar. Even when we consider secular aspirations and goals, your "high calling" may not be your neighbor's "high calling", and theirs may not be their sibling's "high calling", and so on. We each have our own high calling and that is why it is so important to find the breakthrough in every break and also why we must support each other as we advance beyond it. Our individual "high callings" are waiting for us all.

Chapter 9 reminds us to get our breakthroughs because all of us need the wins and none of us are too perfect to never experience a break. This is the sincerity in Paul's confession that I love the most. He is sure that he has a way to go. But he is adamant about his commitment to get there. Against all odds, he is certain to apprehend it. For Paul, to apprehend means to forget what is behind him and reach for what is before him. Ultimately, he presses to reach the mark where the prize of the high calling is. Which means that he has positioned his attention towards a central point and pressed against obstacles with force to advance into his destiny.

When you experience an improvement like a breakthrough, it is an advancement. Although Chapter 7 talked about moving forward (action) and Chapter 8 showed you how (application), this last plea is to help you understand the necessity for repeated breakthroughs (advancement). Every breakthrough is the end of a break, but it does not represent the culmination of your life. There is more.

Resist the temptation to stay in that moment of celebration too long. Resist the temptation to pick up old habits again. Resist the fear of not knowing what the next day might bring.

You must advance! Like a soldier in the field, advance. It is not a mad rush forward. This movement is strategic and intentional.

Beloved, push beyond the break to get your breakthrough and push beyond the breakthrough to achieve your prize. Your high calling is waiting!

Citations

Foster, Richard J. *Celebration of Discipline: The Path to Spiritual Growth*. New York, NY: HarperCollins, 1998.

Hull, Bill. *The Disciple-Making Pastor: Leading Others On the Journey of Faith*. Grand Rapids, MI: Baker Books, 2007.

Tallent, Aaron. "25 Greatest Coaches in NFL History". *Athlon Sports.* Updated 2022. https://athlonsports.com/nfl/25-greatest-head-coaches-nfl-history.

ABOUT THE AUTHOR

Dr. Hayes is fascinated by the way people function in their relationships and how those relationships affect their community. There is so much to gain when you investigate why people do the things they do.

Dr. Kimberly Hayes is a wife, mother, senior pastor, ministry planter, licensed life coach, senior systems engineer, teacher, and a published author with Goshen Publishers.

Prior to her calling in ministry, Dr. Hayes received her BS in Computer Science at North Carolina A&T State University, in Greensboro, NC. Her commitment to continued education led her to complete a Master of Divinity degree in Practical Theology/Church and Ministry in May 2012 as well as a Doctor of Ministry degree in Leadership and Renewal, Ministerial Leadership and Community Transformation in May 2018 at Regent University in Virginia Beach, VA. Dr. Hayes is bi-vocational and currently works as a Senior Systems Engineer for the Johns Hopkins University Applied Physics Lab in Maryland while serving as the Planter and Senior Pastor of Faith Tabernacle of Prayer and Praise COGIC.

Spiritually gifted as an exhorter, a teacher, and with a word of wisdom, Dr. Hayes has walked as a warrior in her office of pastor for over 18 years. She is a discipleship innovator, and the creator and developer of DiscipleMe©, a discipleship application for mobile devices that engage disciples around the world.

While writing and publishing her doctoral dissertation, Dr. Hayes realized that her long-term commitment to the healthy individual and the healthy community required a greater offering. Her first book with

Goshen Publishers, We Collide, was born to reach people where they are despite age, race, economics, relationship status, or religious beliefs to help minimize relational collision and the fatalities that occur because of them. Dr. Hayes' second book, We Break Through, reaches the individual in the middle of their break, wrestling to choose the right path, and perhaps unaware that despite the turbulence, they are still postured for maximum hope and healing.

Having recently launched Thrive! with Dr. Kimberly Hayes, she also provides leadership training, mentoring, spiritual development, and coaching—assisting people to heal, to give, to grow, to help more, to collide less, and break through!

Made in United States
North Haven, CT
21 September 2022

24381907R00096